Comprehension and Data Analysis Questions in Advanced Physics

Comprehension and Data Analysis Questions in Advanced Physics

D. J. Hustings B.Sc., Cert.Ed.
Lecturer in charge of physics
West Bridgford College of Further Education, Nottingham

John Murray 50 Albemarle Street London

To Norma

Text set in 10/11 pt. IBM Press Roman, printed by photo-lithography, and bound in Great Britain at The Pitman Press, Bath

ISBN 0 7195 3208 6

Preface

This book contains a set of exercises in comprehension and data analysis in physics at A-level standard. The comprehension type of paper has been adopted for examining at A-level by the University of London Board, the Joint Matriculation Board and the Nuffield Foundation. A data analysis paper is used in the London Board's examination and many other boards set shorter questions which rely on graphical analysis.

Part One: Comprehension

This section consists of 18 comprehension exercises. No classification is made with regard to subject matter because the topics do not fall neatly under the classical headings of Heat, Light etc., though I have tried to achieve a balance of material. No classification is made with regard to degree of difficulty because this must be subjective in exercises of this kind.

Each exercise contains an abstract from recent scientific literature, followed by a series of questions designed to test and develop the following skills:

(i)   the explanation of various technical words or phrases used in the article,
(ii) the ability to summarize passages in the article and to present the information gathered in a precise, logical and literate fashion,
(iii) the recall of physical principles and their application to the contents of the article,
(iv) the ability to comprehend and interpret diagrams and data, and
(v)   the ability to form opinions and to compare different techniques or theories.

It is the answering technique which needs to be developed because much of the subject matter will be outside a conventional A-level course. The primary objective is that the student should learn to apply his knowledge of physics to novel situations.

Part Two: Data Analysis

A paper of this type has been used since 1973 by the University of London Board and is being considered for use by other boards. All physics teachers should find this section useful in giving students practice in the analysis and interpretation of experimental data.

The topics in this section have been chosen to balance the subject matter of Section One, while at the same time illustrating a wide range of experimental laws. The questions test the ability to manipulate data, to transform equations into linear form and use graphical methods to verify them. The student may also be asked to draw conclusions from the graphs, to criticize the experimental method and to suggest improvements.

I am extremely grateful to the authors, publishers and institutions for permission to use the articles in the Comprehension Section. These articles first appeared in:

New Scientist, London; the weekly review of science and technology.
Nature
Discovery
Physics Bulletin
Electronics and Power
The School Science Review
Atomic and Nuclear Physics by Littlefield and Thorley
    (Van Nostrand).

D.J.H. 1975

Contents

Preface, v

viii   **Contents**

Part One: Comprehension

Hints for answering Comprehension Papers

Before attempting to answer any of the questions read the article through twice: the first time to obtain a general outline of the contents and the second time paying more attention to detail. Answer the questions in the order in which they are set and re-read the sections to which each question refers.

If you are asked to explain the meaning of words or phrases used in the article do so with reference to the context in which they are used; an etymological definition may not be sufficient.

Where you are required to summarize or precis information from the article do so in your own words. You may use concepts and terminology from the passage but you should not simply edit the passage.

Try to relate your general knowledge of physics to the specialized topics which will often be new to you. Illustrate your answers by diagrams or sketch graphs where appropriate and explain clearly any concepts or analogies which you apply.

Do not be afraid to express an opinion about ideas suggested in the article but do justify your criticisms. Write legibly and concisely throughout. Do not give your answers in note form unless specifically instructed to do so, but try to develop a direct coherent style.

1 Adhesion

In the past the forces which make two materials stick to one another have been attributed to a variety of causes including chemical reaction, electrostatic attraction and even mechanical interlocking. I shall discuss only two propositions – the adsorption theory, perhaps the most widely accepted, and the diffusion theory, which is strongly favoured by many Russian workers.

The idea that a layer of adhesive is physically adsorbed on to a surface can be explained by the presence of two forces, both of an electrical origin. The first has been known since the 1930s as the dispersion force and arises, in a sense, because the electrons which orbit an atomic nucleus are never distributed evenly. As a result every atom tends to have two poles, one slightly positive and one slightly negative. The unlike poles of each atom will of course attract each other. The force with which they do so will be very weak – perhaps about one hundred times weaker than the average chemical bond. Nevertheless there is good reason to believe that the dispersion force plays an important role in adhesion, and indeed in cohesion. We now know, for instance, that dispersion forces are largely responsible for binding solid material together across the faults and dislocations that inevitably occur in its crystal structure. Theory shows, however, that the strength of this force decreases as the sixth or seventh power of the distance which separates two atoms.

In practice the situation is a good deal more complicated, for we must deal with the force between two surfaces rather than between two atoms. The relative permittivity of the material will, for one thing, determine the strength of the force. H. B. G. Casimir in the Netherlands and the Soviet scientist, E. M. Lifshitz, have played an important part in extending the theory to cover practical cases. Their conclusions are that in fact the force varies with the fourth power of the distance of separation and this has been confirmed by both Russian and Belgian workers in actual experiments. As we shall see this has an important bearing on an understanding of adhesion.

The dispersion forces are operative over relatively large distances of about one-thousandth of a millimetre. However, there exists a second force which binds materials together much more strongly over much smaller distances. It often happens that the distribution of electrons in a chemical bond is *intrinsically asymmetrical*: in the carbon-chloride bond, for instance, the electron distribution tends to be greater nearer the chlorine atom than the carbon atom. This of course gives rise to an attractive force between unlike poles, but this force differs from the dispersion force in that it is an intrinsic property of the chemical bond, and does not result from a purely random distribution of electrons around the atomic nucleus. However, the force between these polar groups is relatively strong and so they are often introduced into modern adhesives.

Thus we have two forces capable of binding material together — the stronger operating only over very small distances and the weaker capable of bridging flaws equivalent in size to several molecular layers and thus of 'biting deep' across surface irregularities. As we shall see, one of the most difficult problems of adhesion is to bring two surfaces together so closely that these forces become really effective.

The forces we have been discussing so far — together with the more straightforward chemical bonds sometimes formed between surfaces — constitute the basis of the modern theory of adsorption: the idea that molecules of the adhesive are physically adsorbed on to the surface, where they are held by dispersion and polar forces, is now probably the most widely accepted theory of adhesion. It is not, however, the only one.

Some important Russian workers have severely criticized the adsorption theory favoured in the West and believe instead that intimate molecular contact is followed by the diffusion of one chemical species into the other. Most scientists are used to the idea that rubber-like polymers, although solids, behave from the viewpoint of certain thermodynamic properties as if they were liquids. When *miscible liquids* are brought into contact their molecules diffuse into each other until they form a *homogeneous mixture*. A surface of masticated natural rubber brought into contact with another such surface shows such good adhesion that it is impossible ever to separate the two surfaces along their original plane. Both Russian and Western workers believe that in this case some limited form of diffusion has occurred whereby parts of the very large polymer molecules move across the original plane of contact and lose their identity in the mass on the other side. However, Russian workers, notably S. S. Voyutskii, have generalized this phenomenon and, with a considerable weight of evidence, have argued that diffusion is always, or nearly always, involved in adhesion; that, for example, the adhesion of rubber to textile fibres involves some, naturally limited diffusion of parts of the rubber molecule into the *amorphous regions* between the crystallites of the textile fibre; and that the adhesion of epoxy resin to aluminium could involve diffusion of parts of molecules into the interstices between the aluminium oxide crystals forming the aluminium surface.

However, most of the quantitative evidence which has been produced in support of this theory can also be explained as time effects caused by the need for the surfaces to come truly into contact. For this reason, most British workers, and of course some Russian workers, reserve the idea of diffusion for mutually soluble rubbery polymers.

Quite clearly the key to good adhesion – at least as explained by the adsorption theory – is intimate contact between adhesive and *substrate*. Unfortunately this is very difficult to obtain in practice.

Studies of friction between solids have shown how small the area of contact between two smooth surfaces actually is. Figure 1.1 is based on a tracing of the outline of the surface irregularities of a lapped metal surface. If two of

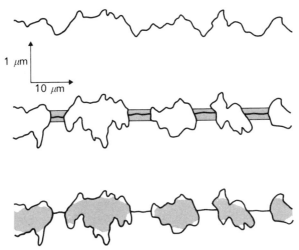

Figure 1.1 Surface roughness of an apparently smooth surface is shown highly magnified (top). This causes quite large cavities to appear if two such surfaces are pressed tightly together (middle). Even adhesives cannot be made to fill these cavities completely (bottom). Intimate molecular contact between surfaces is the key to good adhesion.

these surfaces are brought together, even a light pressure will produce stresses sufficient to flatten and weld together some of the points of contact (see Figure 1.1 centre). When the pressure is removed, the surfaces, which have been *elastically deformed*, tend to spring apart and thus rupture any union that has been formed. It might be thought that an adhesive could fill the irregularities or voids shown in Figure 1.1, but this is difficult because the liquid adhesive must penetrate into these minute cavities but at the same time allow air or vapour to escape from them. Calculation has shown this to be impossible within a reasonably short period of time and probably results in a situation such as that shown in Figure 1.1 (bottom).

When looked at in these terms it is easy to see that adhesion can be thought of as a battle between two opposing variables. On the one hand we have attractive forces that become very weak as separation is increased. And on the other we have surfaces which, when viewed on the same scale of a few millionths of a millimetre, are rough and cannot therefore be brought into extensive and intimate contact. The answer, of course, is to use a liquid adhesive which will make intimate molecular contact with the surface by flowing into the cracks and crevices of the surface. Theory shows, as we might expect, that if the liquid does wet the surface completely the work of adhesion (between liquid and surface) is greater than the work of cohesion (in the liquid). In effect this means that if an adhesive wets the surface effectively, the joint will not fail along the interface of adhesive and surface. This is in accordance with what we find in practice — a fastener glued to the wall, for instance, will invariably bring down the plaster rather than part company with it.

Unfortunately, there is no relation between the energies of adsorption, where these are known, and the strength of the joints formed with the particular combination of metal and adsorbed substance. This is not to say that adsorption is not involved, but that the strength of real joints is determined by the geometry of the stresses involved. The stress acting on a *simple butt joint* is not just a *tensile stress*, but a combination of many others caused by the way the adhesive shrinks as it sets.

However, adsorption is believed to explain the excellence of adhesives, such as epoxy, resorcinol/formaldehyde and other resins which contain hydroxyl groups known to be strongly adsorbed on to metal oxides, the normal surface of metals. Chemisorption has also been evoked, with considerable circumstantial evidence, to explain the effectiveness of certain methods used to bond rubber to metals and to textiles.

(*From an article by W. C. Wake*, Discovery, *Vol. 25, August 1964.*)

Questions

1   Explain the meaning of the following words or phrases as used in the article:
   (a)   intrinsically asymmetrical
   (b)   miscible liquids
   (c)   homogeneous mixture
   (d)   amorphous regions
   (e)   substrate
   (f)   elastically deformed
   (g)   simple butt joint
   (h)   tensile stress

2   Distinguish carefully between the two types of force which can be attributed to the properties of extranuclear electrons.

3   Why does the relative permittivity of a material determine the strength of the dispersion force in that material?

4   What is the difference between absorption and adsorption?

5 Explain the modification made by many Soviet scientists to the adsorption theory favoured in the West.

6 Why is it so difficult to achieve intimate molecular contact between adhesive and substrate?

7 Sketch the appearance, in cross-section, of a drop of liquid on a surface if the angle of contact between liquid and surface is (a) about $30°$, (b) about $150°$. In each sketch label the angle of contact.

8 What is the energy criterion that regulates the strength of the joint between adhesive and substrate?

2 Ceramic structures

An important general property of materials is their strength per unit weight; this is certainly of significance for most ceramic products, whether forming part of a complex structure or the carrying load of a waitress in a restaurant. The latter context is of some significance since many of the available methods of increasing the strength of tableware involve an increase in weight. Table 2.1 shows strength/weight ratios for a range of common materials and indicates that ceramics do not show up too badly.

Table 2.1. Strength/weight ratios for some common materials

Material	Young's modulus E (MN m^{-2})	Bulk density ρ (kg m^{-3})	E/ρ (approx.)
Alumina	35×10^4	3.9×10^3	90
Bone china	8	2.6	31
Glass	7	2.5	28
Aluminium	7	2.7	26
Steel	20	7.8	26
Brick	5	2.2	23
Oak	1.3	0.7	19
Concrete	2.8	2.3	12
Perspex	0.6	1.2	5

Although static strengths are higher than necessary for nearly all purposes, brittleness is a problem wherever impact is likely to be encountered. All ceramic materials are brittle in the sense that they exhibit *linear stress-strain relationships* up to the point of fracture and also in the sense that crack propagation is generally easy and the work of fracture is low. Over a wide range of strengths they fail at a fairly constant level of strain, of the order of 1 part in 1000. Brittleness of course is found only at room temperature. Even so, it is perhaps not sufficiently widely appreciated that even at room temperature *time and relaxation effects* are operative; internal friction is easily measurable in all ceramic materials. Compressive strengths may be from 5 to 10 times as high as tensile strength so that in many circumstances it will be advantageous for designers to ensure that ceramics are used in compression.

The measurement of strength presents many interesting problems which are worthy of detailed discussion in themselves but cannot be dealt with in this paper. Suffice it to say that a *general parameter*, such as Young's modulus, will serve as a good index of strength over a wide range of working conditions. But two very important qualifications need to be recognized. The first is that apparent strength in practice will be as much a function of surface finish as of bulk properties. Surface flaws, especially if they are located at points of maximum stress, can have a devastating effect on realized strength. Secondly, the effective strength of a manufactured product is as much dependent on its shape as on the material from which it is made. To illustrate this point we may note that it is not easy to double the strength of a tableware body by any known technological change but it is possible to increase the chipping resistance of a plate by a factor of 30 by changing the shape of the edge. For those who are interested in the philosophy of measurement and the absolute validity of experimental data it is perhaps worth mentioning that all strength parameters have to be determined on specimens which have a particular shape.

It is now well known that there are three recognizable strength levels for ceramic materials. Theoretical considerations would seem to indicate possible ultimate strengths of the order of 10^4 MN m^{-2}; highest attainable values in practice are 10^3 MN m^{-2}, with a wide range of industrial materials around 10^2 MN m^{-2} or less. Expressed another way, theoretical strengths are around $E/10$ but strengths in practice may be as low as $E/1000$ for many materials in common use. To understand the strength characteristics of commercial ceramic products it is necessary to appreciate the materials and processes involved in their manufacture. By far the largest proportion of them are in the clay based system, though an important category, namely basic refractories, has its own special features. Clay based ceramics are compounded of clay, some *fluxing material* and a crystalline material frequently referred to as a filler. When this combination is mixed together and fired. the resulting material may be regarded as consisting of four components:

(1) the filler, which may have remained unaltered during the firing;
(2) the glass, which has been formed from the melting of the flux and which serves either to bind the filler particles together at the points of contact or to form *a continuous matrix* in which the crystalline matter is embedded;
(3) the pores, which derive mainly from the *interstices* between the constituent particles; and
(4) the cracks, which may be in the filler as a result of grinding or in the glass or filler as a result of *thermal mismatch*.

All these four components are significant in the study of the factors affecting the strength of the product.

The glassy phase is usually an alkali aluminosilicate, the composition of which cannot be altered easily. The amount is variable from one product to another, being as high as 40 per cent in some vitreous bodies and as low as 10 per cent in some porous bodies. More glass usually means higher strength but it also increases brittleness since it is the glassy phase that most readily encourages crack propagation.

The filler, which may be present in proportions varying from 20 to 50 per cent, is important in two main senses: it plays a key role in the development of flaws and it offers a practical means of controlling the elastic properties of the system. Crystalline silica, in the form of either quartz or cristobalite, is frequently used as a filler, mainly because it has a high thermal expansion and thus facilitates glazing. But this high thermal expansion, together with the high volume changes associated with the structural inversions, results in a serious thermal mismatch and in an associated flaw system. It is this flaw system that is largely responsible for low strength. Since the flaw dimension is related to the grain size of the filler there is here a means of controlling the strength. It turns out that over a wide range of industrial ceramics, in quite complex systems, the well-known power law applies, the strength being inversely proportional to the grain size to the power of about one half. It is thus possible to bring about significant strength increases by decreasing the grain size, although there are limits to this. At very low sizes *solution effects* appear to lower the strength again. In practice decreasing the grain size of the filler from 50 to 10 μm could increase the strength by about 100 per cent. The nature of the filler is also important. When silica is replaced by alumina, for example, the thermal mismatch is reduced, flaws are minimized and the effective *Young's modulus of the system* is increased. An interesting successful application of this is in the strong tableware bodies containing alumina coming increasingly on to the market.

Many industrial ceramics have a volume porosity which may be as high as 30 per cent and even those which have no accessible pores may have closed pores occupying 50 per cent of the volume or more. The effect of this porosity on strength has been measured for a wide range of materials and it turns out that the results fit very well the kind of exponential relationship that has been established for simple single-phase systems. The practical significance of this is reflected in the fact that, for example, bone china is often twice as strong as earthenware. The penalty that has to be endured, of course, is an increase in weight.

Although most materials used as fillers are roughly equant in shape there are some that are crystallized in the form of long thin needles. When these are aligned parallel to each other they can act effectively as barriers to cracks propagating in a direction at right angles, and this kind of orientation arises in a number of commonly-used making processes. Unfortunately it is scarcely ever possible to produce orientation in the most favourable direction; hence the limited application of ceramic fibres for this purpose.

The effect of glazing on the strength of ceramics is worth a mention. Partly as a result of sealing up surface flaws and partly on account of the compression derived from thermal expansion differences, appreciable strength increases, up to double, can be achieved. Further increases by the use of very high glaze compression are not usually attainable because of the inability of the body to withstand the corresponding internal tension. Where the body is of such a nature that this tension can be resisted, very high strengths can be achieved, as for example with glass-ceramic tableware.

(*From an article by A. Dinsdale in* Physics Bulletin, *November 1972. Used with the permission of the Institute of Physics.*)

Questions

1 Explain the meaning of the following words or phrases as used in the article:
   (a) linear stress-strain relationships
   (b) time and relaxation effects
   (c) a general parameter
   (d) fluxing material
   (e) a continuous matrix
   (f) interstices
   (g) thermal mismatch
   (h) solution effects
   (i) Young's modulus of the system

2 Give examples of instances in which strength per unit weight of a ceramic material would be of more importance than its absolute strength.

3 How would you qualify the statement that 'all ceramic materials are brittle'?

4 Distinguish between compressive strength and tensile strength.

5 Explain the effect of the composition of the glassy phase on the final strength of a ceramic material.

6 Summarize the ways in which the filler can determine the properties of the final product.

7 Write an equation with strength as a function of grain size, naming the symbols used.

3 New law for liquids: Don't snap, stretch!

Old-timers in the shipyards on the Clyde still tell the tale of an epoch-making ship that was launched in the days of Queen Victoria. Fitted with a new type of steam propulsion, the ship had propellors designed to turn faster than any propellors had turned before. This ship was going to be a world-beater. But, alas, it didn't work out quite like that. When the propellors were driven beyond a certain speed the ship slowed down instead of speeding up. And when she was eventually examined in dry dock, her propellors looked as if they had been nibbled by a pack of metal-eating mice.

Although this particular vessel is something of a legend, compounded out of experiences gained on a whole series of early propeller-driven ships, the story summarizes the discovery of what came to be known as 'cavitation'. In most types of rotating hydraulic machinery, as the speed is increased, pressures at the trailing edges of moving blades gradually fall. Eventually a speed is reached at which the pressure, somewhere, falls to the vapour pressure of the liquid. Then the fun starts. The liquid at this point begins to boil and bubble as cavities appear. But they are very short-lived because they are soon swept into a region of higher pressure, where they collapse with (literally) a bang, which damages the metal in the immediate vicinity.

These three consequences of cavitation – loss of efficiency, noise, and metal erosion – are so serious that they impose a limitation on the speed at which hydraulic machinery can operate. In a world where speed is almost a god, it is not surprising that a great deal of research effort is directed at overcoming cavitation. The effort takes several different forms depending on the research discipline.

The hydrodynamicist's approach is to design his machinery so as to reduce the tendency to cavitate, and to ensure that when cavitation does occur both the loss of efficiency and the erosion effect are minimized. One interesting development is the so-called 'supercavitating' pump, which cavitates furiously but throws its bubbles well clear of the pump blades, so that they collapse without doing any damage.

The metallurgist's method is to study the phenomenon of erosion by bubble collapse, and to develop new alloys or coatings with improved erosion resistance. This work has led to modern hydraulic machines which can withstand cavitating conditions for much longer periods than earlier equipment.

The physicist adopts a more fundamental approach, inquiring why liquids begin to cavitate and whether they can be prevented from doing so. This article is mainly concerned with these fundamental questions, and especially with the light thrown upon them by recent developments at the National Engineering Laboratory.

Although it is more than 100 years since Berthelot first showed that liquids have a relatively high tensile strength, very few people, even in scientific circles, seem to be aware of this. Because it takes no effort to put a hand into a basin of water and pull out a handful of the unresisting fluid, many scientists and technologists instinctively believe that water 'obviously' has no tensile strength. What they forget is that under such circumstances liquids fall under shear (that is, by molecules sliding sideways past one another) and not under tension (that is, by the molecules moving directly away from one another). And it is, of course, true that *liquids have no shear strength*.

To see whether liquids really do have a tensile strength, it is necessary to create conditions where pure hydrostatic tension can be developed, free from shear stresses. The easiest way to achieve this is to repeat Berthelot's original experiment. The sceptic can do this easily with a minimum of apparatus in the following way.

Take a short length of thick-walled glass capillary tube, seal one end in a flame and fill it almost full of liquid. Then seal the other end in a flame, taking care to leave the smallest possible air space in the tube. Place the sealed tube in a beaker of water and gradually heat it. The liquid will expand, dissolving the air remaining in the tube as it does so. For some time there will be no sign of an air bubble, although the cooling liquid 'wants' to contract. The water, having wetted the whole of the inside wall of the tube, adheres to it, and instead of contracting the water will remain in a stretched condition under a uniform tensile stress. Suddenly there will be an audible click and an air bubble will reappear as the water eventually fractures under the increasing tensile stress.

By making a more elaborate type of Berthelot tube out of stainless steel and fitting *strain gauges* to its outside wall, we can measure the negative pressure inside the tube. Tensions of about −20 atmospheres have been measured in this way at NEL.

Much higher negative pressures can be generated by the use of a centrifuge. By rotating a Z-shaped capillary tube filled with liquid, the late Dr Lyman Briggs at the US National Bureau of Standards generated negative pressure in the region of −300 atm in a number of liquids, so establishing a world record that has remained unbroken now for 20 years.

As liquids can be made to withstand high negative pressure in hydrostatic laboratory tests, is there any prospect of making them do so inside hydraulic machinery, instead of cavitating? At present, the prospect looks remote. But it would be wrong to dismiss the idea.

In most engineering applications, cavitation begins with a bubble large enough to be seen by the naked eye. Wherever large quantities of water are in motion near a free surface — around the stern of a ship or at the intake to a hydroelectric generating system, for instance — the water is likely to be peppered with bubbles. It only needs one such bubble to be swept into a region of slight negative pressure for a cavity to be formed; this cavity will then break up and beget other bubbles, which will grow into subsequent cavities, and so *ad infinitum*.

But there are a few situations where machinery operates in liquids that might be expected to be entirely free from bubbles. The solubility of a gas in a liquid increases in proportion to its pressure. Consequently, bubbles should dissolve very rapidly at great depths. Even without a high hydrostatic pressure small bubbles should dissolve rapidly because surface tension greatly increases the gas pressure inside a very small bubble. Hence there should be no bubbles in the depths of a large body of liquid — and yet the propellors of submarines and pumps drawing from the bottom of large storage tanks can still cavitate.

One reason for this is that undissolved gas nuclei of microscopic size exist in water, and these nuclei grow into bubbles as soon as negative pressures are encountered. We still do not know for certain just how the gas in these micronuclei manages to escape being forced into solution. But a lot of experimental evidence suggest that these gas nuclei are stabilized by being held in *hydrophobic crevices* in solid surfaces. The solid surfaces concerned may be either boundary surfaces or tiny specks of dirt suspended in the liquid. As the illustration (Figure 3.1) shows, if a crevice is hydrophobic the curvature

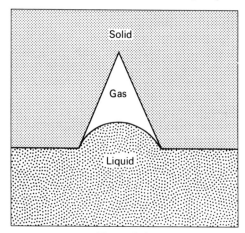

Figure 3.1

of the meniscus will be convex towards the trapped gas, and in this case surface tension will reduce the pressure of the gas, instead of increasing it as in an ordinary bubble.

Nuclei of this kind normally occur in both natural waters and distilled water. They are stable indefinitely at pressures a little above atmospheric, but are soon destroyed by the application of higher pressures. Artificial nuclei have recently been produced by treating fine powders with silicone water-repellants. These are much more stable at high pressures than any naturally occurring nuclei. Their behaviour provides further experimental confirmation of the hydrophobic crevice theory of stabilization.

(*From an article entitled 'New Law for Liquids: Don't Snap, Stretch!' by A. T. J. Hayward, New Scientist, Vol. 45, No 686, 29 January 1970.*)

Questions

1   Explain the meaning of the following words or phrases as used in the article:
   (a)   liquids have no shear strength
   (b)   strain gauges
   (c)   hydrophobic crevices

2   Describe how cavitation can seriously limit the performance of hydraulic machinery.

3   What methods have been employed by engineers to reduce the effects of cavitation?

4   Distinguish carefully, with the aid of diagrams, between shear stress and tensile stress.

5   Discuss whether the water in Berthelot's experiment is completely free from shear stresses during the cooling process.

6   In what sense can the phrase 'negative pressure' be used to describe the state of the water in Berthelot's experiment?

7   Summarize the theories proposed to explain the onset of cavitation in water.

8   With reference to Figure 3.1, explain why the pressure in the gas bubble is lower than that in the surrounding liquid.

4 Theories of Creation

The visible universe, Hamlet's 'brave o'erhanging firmament, this majestical roof fretted with golden fire', has always been a subject for poetry. Although today we have no Shakespeare to translate into verse the facts discovered by modern astronomy, these facts, even when plainly stated, have an eloquence of their own. One fact that we now fully appreciate is that a single glance at the heavens gives us a view of cosmic objects observed at all different epochs in the history of the universe. This effect occurs because the finite speed of light causes us to see other parts of the universe, not as they are now, but as they were in the past: light from the sun, for example, takes about eight minutes to reach the earth, which means that we see the sun as it was eight minutes ago; similarly, the nearest bright star, Alpha Centauri, is seen by us as it was four years ago, and is said to be four light years distant. (*One light year is equivalent to about ten million million kilometres.*) Although we may not have a privileged position in the universe in the sense understood before the time of Copernicus, it is essential that we describe the universe relative to our own point in space and time, for that is the only point from which we can make our observations.

As we penetrate further out into space with our observations, we necessarily penetrate further back in time. What we see in the heavens is in reality a panorama in both space and time — a vast array of cosmic objects which, being at all different distances, are consequently being seen at all different epochs.

The most striking feature of all the clusters of galaxies outside our own local group is that they appear to be receding from us. By analysing the light from these galaxies with a spectroscope, we may identify characteristic features of the chemical elements, and determine if the source of light is moving relative to ourselves. Studying galaxies in this way Hubble, in the 1930s, came to the conclusion that the farther galaxies are away from us, the faster they appear to be receding, and that *distance and speed of recession are proportional*: this is the famous result known as Hubble's law. As an extreme example, the cluster of galaxies in the constellation of Hydra, at about one thousand million light years distance (which represents the limit of observation for the two-hundred-inch telescope), has a speed of recession which is about one-tenth of the speed of light itself.

The generally accepted conclusion from these observations is that the universe, the sum total of all the clusters of galaxies and the space in between them, is expanding. The observed motion of the rest of the universe away from us is only relative, and can be regarded as the effect of having an expanding space in which the clusters of galaxies are located. (By analogy, in the case of a rubber balloon being inflated, each point on the surface is moving away from every other point, so that an observer situated anywhere on the surface would see every point as receding from him.) Of all the mysteries of the observable universe, this expansion is one of the most mysterious; it also has some very remarkable consequences.

If the universe is expanding then we might well ask in what kind of state it all began. One theory of the origin of the universe, put forward by Lemaitre and discussed further by Gamow, is that in the beginning there was a 'big bang', which sent all the *primeval material* flying outwards from a very confined region of space. If we know the distances and speeds of recession of all the clusters of galaxies, it is possible to calculate, assuming the big bang theory, the time at which the bang occurred: that moment of time, at which the universe began to evolve, was about ten thousand million years ago. But if, 'in the beginning', there was a big bang, what happened before 'time zero'? Such a thought, following from the interpretation of the theory using traditional concepts, seems to lead straight into the realm of metaphysics, and was therefore unwelcome to most astronomers.

An alternative theory, put forward in 1948 by Hoyle, and by Bondi and Gold, is called the theory of continuous creation. According to this theory the universe, instead of having been created in one event of unimaginable energy, is being created all the time. As the universe expands, atoms of material appear out of nowhere to fill the extra space that results from the expansion, maintaining the overall density constant. The advantages of this process are that it can go on indefinitely, and that there exists no 'time zero', which would demand further explanation. To any observer the universe always appears the same, from any point of observation and at any epoch of time, and so is said to be in a 'steady state'. The theory unfortunately has the disadvantage that the process by which atoms or more basic particles appear is not known from laboratory studies, and is actually forbidden by the well-established laws of elementary particle physics: it is surprising that this did not deter astronomers from accepting the steady state (continuous creation) theory, especially as elementary particle physics was at that time enjoying an exceptionally high reputation.

In very recent years it has been possible to make a tentative choice between the two rival theories of the origin of the universe — big bang or steady state. A crucial piece of evidence has come from observations of radio galaxies made by Ryle and Clarke with the large radio interferometer at Cambridge. If the steady state theory were true, then no matter how far one looked out into space, and therefore back in time, the universe should always appear the same. In fact, the radio observations have shown that this is not so: the universe appears to have been in a state of greater density (that is, with the galaxies more congested) in the past than it is now, a state of affairs that is definitely in disagreement with the steady state theory. The big bang theory, on the other hand, predicts that the overall density of the universe should progressively decrease with time.

There is another piece of evidence in favour of the big bang theory. If the universe did in fact begin in a very dense state, and with sufficient energy for the galaxies to be hurled out into space with their observed speeds, then it must have been very hot indeed in its initial moments. Radiation produced at this stage would have had an energy that can be calculated, and the effect of the subsequent expansion of the universe on this radiation can also be calculated: from such considerations it may be concluded that, after the estimated time from the initial moment until the present day, the radiation should fill the whole of space and be in the form of micro- (short radio) waves. A microwave background radiation from space was discovered in 1965, by Penzias and Wilson at the Bell Telephone Laboratories, and was immediately identified with the hypothetical radiation remaining from the big bang. The protagonists of the steady state theory have suggested other causes of this radiation, but so far the arguments put forward have not been entirely convincing. The big bang theory may be nearer the truth.

(*From an article entitled 'Man's View of the Universe', by David F. Falla,* School Science Review, *Vol. 53, September 1971. Used with the permission of The Association for Science Education.*)

Questions

1   Explain the meaning of the following words or phrases as used in the article:
   (a)   one light year is equivalent to about ten million million kilometres
   (b)   distance and speed of recession are proportional
   (c)   the primeval material

2   What is the reason for the statement that our view of the heavens is a panorama in space and time?

3   Why do no two elements exhibit the same emission spectrum?

4   Explain carefully how spectroscopic evidence (sometimes called 'the red shift') leads to the conclusion that the universe is expanding and to Hubble's law.

5   Discuss the concept of the beginning of time in terms of the big bang theory and the steady state theory.

6   It is stated in the article that the continuous creation aspect of the steady state theory is forbidden by the laws of elementary particle physics.

Discuss the implications of this, and give your views on creation and the laws of physics with respect to both the big bang and steady state theories.

7 Summarize the details of the two pieces of evidence which are in favour of the big bang theory.

5 Nature and origin of cosmic rays

Primary cosmic rays have their origin somewhere out in space. They travel with speeds almost as great as the speed of light and can be deflected by planetary or intergalactic magnetic fields. They are unique in that a single particle can have an energy as great as 10^{19} eV but the collective energy is only about 10 microwatts per square metre for cosmic rays entering the atmosphere, which is roughly equal to the energy of starlight. In starlight the energy of a single photon is only a few electron volts compared with the average for cosmic rays of 6 GeV per particle.

The composition of cosmic rays entering the earth's atmosphere is fairly well known from balloon experiments and it is found that these primary cosmic rays consist mainly of fast *protons*. There are very few *positrons*, electrons or photons, and the particle composition is mainly 92 per cent protons, 7 per cent alpha-particles and 1 per cent 'heavy' nuclei, carbon, nitrogen, oxygen, neon, magnesium, silicon, iron, cobalt and nickel stripped of their electrons. The average energy of the cosmic ray flux is 6 GeV, with a maximum of about 10^{10} GeV (compare this with 300 GeV, the maximum energy of artificially accelerated particles). The radiation reaching the earth is almost completely *isotropic*.

As soon as the primary rays enter the earth's atmosphere multiple collisions readily take place with atmospheric atoms producing a large number of secondary particles in showers. Thus when a primary photon strikes an oxygen or nitrogen nucleus a *nuclear cascade* results. These secondary atmospheric radiations contain many new particles, neutral and ionized, as well as penetrating photons, but little if any of the primary radiation survives at sea-level. Secondary cosmic rays consist of about 75 per cent muons and about 25 per cent electrons and positrons, although some alpha-particles, gamma photons and neutrons may be present in negligible quantities.

The collision cross-sections for the primary component of cosmic rays are of the order of 10^{-1} barns and the *mean free path* for a collision process at the top of the atmosphere may be as high as several kilometres. The new particles produced after primary collisions give in their turn more secondary radiations by further collisions until a cascade of particles has developed, increasing in intensity towards the earth. At lower intensities the cosmic ray intensity is not constant with time but depends on the activity of the sun. It is found that during periods of high sunspot activity the cosmic ray intensity is low, presumably due to the trapping of the charged primaries high above the earth by the increased magnetic field of the sun at these times. Corresponding to the 11-year cycle of maximum sunspot activity there is therefore a cycle of minimum cosmic ray intensity.

A recent observation on cosmic ray intensities showed that the sun itself must actually be the source of at least some of the low energy primaries, since at the time of solar flares the cosmic ray intensity increased. However, this can only account for a small fraction of the total, and since cosmic rays are nearly isotropic around the earth their origin in such a 'point source' as the sun is precluded and we must look much further into the depths of space.

An interesting feature of the composition of the primary rays is the existence of heavy nuclides up to atomic masses of about 60, and the fact that the distribution of the elements in cosmic rays shows a similar trend to that in the sun, stars, nebulae and in the non-volatile parts of meteorites, although the primary cosmic radiations are significantly richer in heavy nuclei compared with the general matter of the universe. This seems to indicate a cosmic ray origin in which matter is present and where the conditions are of relatively low energy (compared with cosmic ray energies) possibly in supernovae explosions.

Fermi suggested that the cosmic rays have their origin in *interstellar space* and are accelerated to high energies, as they stream through the arms of a galaxy, by the associated galactic magnetic field which is about 1 nT. The cosmic ray particle is injected into the galactic magnetic field from the surface of a star with an appreciable initial energy and is caused to spiral in this field. It will eventually 'collide' with another region of high magnetic field which is approaching it with a high velocity. The cosmic ray particle is reflected or repelled with increased energy since the magnetic field is moving towards it. When a cosmic ray particle is trapped between two such fields it gains energy by multiple repulsions and the more energetic particles of the distribution finally escape into space with a high velocity of projection. The trapping and ejecting mechanism can be repeated until the particle reaches the solar system where it is observed.

It is concluded, therefore, that cosmic rays acquire their energies in the vicinity of magnetically active stars, especially supernovae. This is supported by the observations on *radio stars* which show intense radio noise due to very fast electrons moving in magnetic fields, suggesting that cosmic rays may also be associated with stellar events of great violence. Since the cosmic rays are pushed about in all directions by these great belts of stellar magnetic fields, in which they undergo multiple reflections and changes of direction, they surround the earth isotropically so that the earth can be regarded as a simple body in a whole sea of cosmic rays.

(*From* Atomic and Nuclear Physics *by T. A. Littlefield and N. Thorley,* Van Nostrand, 1968.)

Questions

1 Explain the meaning of the following words or phrases as used in the article:
   (a) protons
   (b) positrons
   (c) isotropic
   (d) nuclear cascade
   (e) mean free path
   (f) interstellar space
   (g) radio stars

2 Explain why little if any of the primary cosmic radiation survives at sea level.

3 Draw a diagram to represent a nuclear cascade and mark on it the main components of the primary and secondary radiation.

4 Define the electron volt as a unit of energy. Given that the electronic charge is 1.6×10^{-19} C, calculate in joules the average energy per particle in the primary flux.

5 What is the connection between cosmic ray intensity and sunspot activity?

6 Why does the isotropic nature of the cosmic rays around the earth preclude the possibility of the sun being the major source of the radiation?

7 Discuss Fermi's theory of the origin of the cosmic rays and explain the importance of the observations on radio stars.

6 Nuclear fusion reactions

Because of the initial high temperatures required for fusion, estimated at about 10^8 K, the atoms are fully ionized and these ions and the free electrons are moving about very rapidly. It is possible that the separation of positive nuclei and free electrons is never very large because of their electrostatic attraction but they do move much more independently of each other than at ordinary temperatures. The mixture is still electrically neutral, of course, and the whole state is called the plasma state, a sort of second gaseous state. The matter contained in stars and galaxies is largely in the plasma state but the setting up of a plasma in the laboratory requires artificial conditions such as the passage of a heavy electrical discharge through the gas – approaching 1 MA, at which current the *Joule heating* is sufficient to give the particles sufficient kinetic energy to cause fusion to take place.

There are four feasible hydrogen reactions, all of which probably take place in a hydrogen plasma. These are:

$${}_1^2\text{H} + {}_1^2\text{H} \rightarrow {}_2^3\text{He} + {}_0^1\text{n} + 3.25 \text{ MeV} \qquad (1)$$

$${}_1^2\text{H} + {}_1^2\text{H} \rightarrow {}_1^3\text{H} + {}_1^1\text{H} + 4.0 \text{ MeV} \qquad (2)$$

$${}_1^3\text{H} + {}_1^2\text{H} \rightarrow {}_2^4\text{He} + {}_0^1\text{n} + 17.6 \text{ MeV} \qquad (3)$$

$${}_1^2\text{H} + {}_2^3\text{He} \rightarrow {}_2^4\text{He} + {}_1^1\text{H} + 18.3 \text{ MeV} \qquad (4)$$

We notice here that the simplest fusion reaction:

$${}_1^2\text{H} + {}_1^2\text{H} \rightarrow {}_2^4\text{He} + Q$$

does not proceed owing to non-conservation of linear and angular momentum between the three particles. However, the ${}_2^4\text{He}$ nucleus can be regarded as the compound nucleus for the first two reactions quoted, in each case yielding the products shown above.

Thus the four reactions are simply rearrangements and possibly the word 'fusion', in its narrowest sense, is a misnomer. The reactions (3) and (4) of the above are really between the reaction products of (1) and (2) so that in fact we could imagine the overall conversion of six deuterons as follows:

$$6 \, {}_1^2\text{H} \rightarrow 2 \, {}_2^4\text{He} + 2 \, {}_0^1\text{n} + 43 \text{ MeV}$$

This is equivalent to the production of about 10^5 kWh per gram of *deuterium* as compared with about 10^4 kWh per gram of $^{235}_{92}$U in fission, a useful increase.

In the above reactions when there are only two product particles the lighter particles carry away the majority of the energy, so that in the first reaction the neutron takes with it three-quarters of the reaction energy, i.e. about 2.4 MeV and so could be detected as a fast neutron.

Ultimately we require the thermonuclear reaction to be self-sustaining and energy producing. This can only be possible if the rate of generation of energy exceeds the rate of loss at all times. When these are just balanced the plasma is in a critical state, or at a critical temperature which must be exceeded for the reaction to proceed. Energy is lost from the plasma largely by means of X-rays and *bremsstrahlung* and these unavoidable losses set the minimum critical temperature, which for a hydrogen plasma is about 10^8 K.

Thus, if we can heat the hydrogen in an evacuated chamber to this temperature and prevent it reaching the chamber walls where it would lose further energy by conduction, it might be possible to create a *self-sustaining nuclear fusion chain reaction*. This is by no means easy and some of the problems associated with this will now be discussed.

(i) Containment. This is the problem of holding the plasma away from the vessel walls for long enough for fusion to occur, at 10^8 K. In the case of stellar thermonuclear energy, the contraction under gravity when the reaction slows down is sufficient to raise the temperature and pressure again to speed up the reaction. A star is therefore a self-controlled system.

The only method of containment which is feasible at present in the laboratory, is the 'magnetic bottle' method, where the movement of the plasma, which is of course electrically conducting, is controlled by a magnetic field. This may be produced by the passage of the heavy heating current, of the order of a million amperes, down the tube. This produces a circular magnetic field which then reacts with the plasma to 'pinch' it down to a thin filament. This is analogous to two parallel wires with currents in the same direction being drawn together as a result of the left-hand motor rule and is called the 'pinch effect' (see Figure 6.1).

Another method is to maintain a high frequency alternating magnetic field inside a cavity containing the plasma. The plasma is ionized and the reaction with the field causes the plasma to contract under the influence of the 'magnetic pressure'. A third method shown in Figure 6.2 is to use magnetic coils to provide a reflecting region for the moving ions. This is the basis of the so-called mirror machine in which the *lines of magnetic flux are inhomogeneous* and most of the charged particles on reaching M_1 or M_2 will be reflected. Axial particles will be lost so that the plasma would gradually die away.

(ii) Instability of plasma. Ideally the contained plasma is in a continuous line filament. In practice, due to magnetic and electrostatic leakages, the

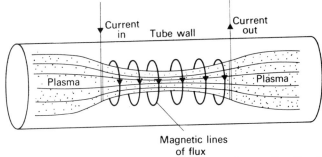

Figure 6.1 Principle of pinch effect in hot plasma. In practice the electric current is induced in the conducting plasma.

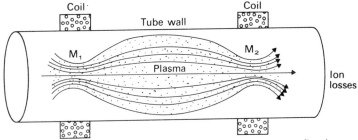

Figure 6.2 Mirror machine with ions trapped between two reflecting regions of converging magnetic fields.

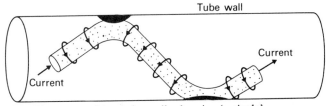

Figure 6.3 Plasma touching tube walls showing 'wriggle'.

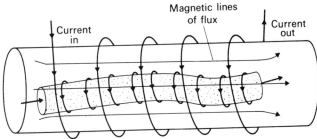

Figure 6.4 'Wriggle' straightened out by stabilizing magnetic field along tube axis.

plasma filament is very distorted, giving rise to the well-known wriggle shown in Figure 6.3. This snake-like effect can only be reduced by a series of correctly placed magnetic fields. Generally the wriggle can be straightened out by the use of an axial magnetic field as shown in Figure 6.4.

(iii) Reaction times. Having contained the plasma and heated it to the right temperature it must now be maintained long enough in these conditions for the nuclei to react. The holding time required depends on the density of the plasma but the time taken for the field to rise to its final value must be much smaller. Some relevant figures are about 1 tesla for a holding time of 0.1 to 1.0 second or 10 tesla for 1 to 10 seconds, where *the field 'rise time'* must be only about 100 microseconds. This involves many difficult engineering problems of storing, switching and transmitting electrical energy of many megajoules during these short pulses. Thus in Zeta (the UKAEA fusion device at Harwell) the capacitor bank was about 1600 μF with working potentials up to 25 kV, giving a stored energy of 0.5 MJ discharged at 50 kA for 3 ms.

Many experimental arrangements have overcome some of the above difficulties on a small scale. The names of Zeta and Sceptre in England and Perhapsatron and Stellarator in the USA are associated with projects of this nature. At present there is no possible way of extracting the fusion energy usefully and it will be many years before the fusion reactor will be a reality. But it will come, and the possibility of extracting the electrical energy directly from the conducting plasma without having the usual turbo-generator is a possibility which makes research in controlled thermonuclear reactions of prime concern. This goal has stimulated work in a whole new field of physics which is now being called magnetoplasma-dynamics, and the fact that many symposia have been held in the United States and also in Western Europe on this single subject points to its technological importance in our search for more power.

(From Atomic and Nuclear Physics *by T. A. Littlefield and N. Thorley, Van Nostrand, 1968.)*

Questions

1   Explain the meaning of the following words or phrases as used in the article:
   (a)   Joule heating
   (b)   deuterium
   (c)   *bremsstrahlung*
   (d)   self-sustaining nuclear fusion chain reaction
   (e)   the lines of magnetic flux are inhomogeneous
   (f)   the field 'rise time'

2   Describe the state of matter referred to as a plasma. In what sense can it be regarded as a second gaseous state?

3 Verify that the reaction representing the overall conversion of six deuterons does follow from the four basic reactions.

4 Define the quantity 'binding energy' and explain how this concept can be used to account for the energy released in a reaction such as (1) in the article. Confirm that the energy released in reaction (1) is equal to 3.25 MeV given the following data:

Mass of $^2_1$H nuclide = 2.014 102 m_u

Mass of $^3_2$He nuclide = 3.016 030 m_u

Mass of neutron = 1.008 665 m_u

1 m_u = 931 MeV

5 Verify that the 43 MeV produced by the conversion of six deuterons is equivalent to about 10^5 kWh per gram of deuterium. (Avogadro constant = 6.023 x 10^{23} mol^{-1}, electronic charge = 1.6 x 10^{-19} C.)

6 What are the main problems associated with the production and control of the plasma?

7 Describe as clearly as you can the operation of the pinch effect, and explain why the pinch effect is, alone, unable to prevent plasma 'wriggle'.

8 Large-scale fusion reactors are still a long way off. Mention two other possible sources of world power which do not depend on traditional fossil fuels (e.g. coal, oil, gas) and discuss the possibilities of one of them in detail.

7 Basic experiments planned with trapped neutrons

The neutron, one of the main constituents of atomic nuclei, is an extremely difficult particle to study. Possessing no electric charge and a small magnetic moment, it cannot be contained by electric or magnetic fields. To complicate things, neutrons can participate in nuclear reactions with container walls or diffuse right through them.

In the late 1950s the Russian physicist Ya B. Zel'dovich calculated that very slow *ultra-cold neutrons* could be contained in a box of carbon or any material of the same density. Their velocity was five metres per second or less. As the probability for the neutrons to interact with atoms in the wall is *inversely proportional* to velocity, Zel'dovich calculated that neutrons could be contained for 10^5 seconds, or about one day (*Soviet Physics JETP*, Vol. 9, p. 1389).

The basic experimental equipment and the theoretical ideas are quite simple (see Figure 7.1). The set up of V. I. Lushchikov, Yu N. Pokotilovskii,

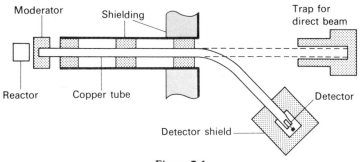

Figure 7.1

A. V. Strelkor and F. J. Shapiro of the Joint Institute for Nuclear Research, Dubna, is shown in the diagram (*JETP Letters*, Vol. 9, p. 23). Neutrons from the reactor passed through a *moderator* which, on the average, slowed them to *thermal velocities* of about 1000 metres per second. The neutrons then entered an evacuated copper tube of length 10.5 metres and diameter 9.4 centimetres. The copper pipe was bent and cleaned with acid. Some of the neutrons have slow velocities and, according to the theory of *wave-particle duality*, those with slow velocities have long wavelengths prohibiting them from diffusing between the copper nuclei at the bend. All neutrons with velocities below 5.7 metres per second were reflected. Thermal neutrons have velocities of approximately 1000 metres per second and most of them went through the tube into the trap.

Lushchikov and his co-workers calculated that they trapped about 1000 neutrons per square centimetre per second. This is too small for useful experiments but the apparatus has not been *optimized*. Most interest centres on the search for an electric dipole moment of the neutron. Experimenters are also aiming at precision measurements of the neutron's lifetime. A free neutron decays to a proton, an electron, and an antineutrino with a *half-life* of over ten minutes. There is disagreement between present measurements of the lifetime and this fundamental property of one of nature's basic particles has eluded precision determination. Hopefully, trapped ultra-cold neutrons will supply the answer.

(*From an article in* New Scientist, *Vol. 44, No. 679, 11 December 1969.*)

Questions

1   Explain the meaning of the following words or phrases as used in the article:
   (a)   ultra-cold neutrons
   (b)   inversely proportional
   (c)   moderator
   (d)   thermal velocities
   (e)   wave-particle duality
   (f)   optimized
   (g)   half-life

2   Explain briefly why it is so difficult to trap free neutrons or to control their behaviour (e.g. speed and direction).

3   The Soviet physicists made their 'neutron guide' by relying on the wave properties of neutrons; ultra-cold neutrons are reflected at the bend in the tube and thermal neutrons diffuse through the wall. What are the main criteria which decide whether any type of wave (e.g. electromagnetic) will penetrate a surface or be reflected by it?

4   Given that Planck's constant, h, is 6.63×10^{-34} J s, and the rest mass of a neutron is 1.67×10^{-27} kg, use the de Broglie equation to compare the wavelengths of ultra-cold neutrons and thermal neutrons with speeds of 5 m s^{-1} and 1000 m s^{-1} respectively.

5   Write an equation to illustrate the decay of a neutron to a proton and an electron. By comparing the charge and mass numbers on both sides of your equation, what can you deduce about the third particle which is formed, the antineutrino?

8 The acoustic surface wave

The acoustic surface wave, or elastic wave, also known after its first, inspired observer as the Rayleigh wave, is already used in materials testing, and the classical mathematical description of its properties can be traced back to *seismology*, but the latest field of application is in a completely new type of electronic circuitry.

The surface wave *propagates* along a solid surface in a similar manner to ripples along the surface of a pond, but with the important difference that the surface particles rotate in an elliptical orbit in the opposite direction to the travelling wave. The surface agitation dies away rapidly into the solid. The result of this and other factors is a wave confined to a narrow surface region, travelling a little slower than a bulk wave with small *attenuation* or scattering, and without any dispersion into its constituent frequencies.

These properties, plus the key fact that the waves travel some hundred thousand times slower than *electromagnetic waves*, is the reason for their appeal to the electronics engineer. If he can transmit electronic signals as surface waves, he can perform signal processing functions in a tiny chip of material that at present require bulky circuit elements on an entirely different scale to modern micro-circuitry. A surface wave travels just one centimetre in the time an electromagnetic wave travels along one half mile of cable, and delay lines are thus bulky pieces of equipment. By using surface wave processing, delay lines (indeed, any piece of circuitry in which signals are to be delayed, compressed, or filtered out of other electromagnetic perturbations) can be produced as tiny planar devices and integrated with the rest of modern micro-circuitry.

This important advance in electronics, variously known as *praetersonics*, *microsound* or *microwave acoustics*, has been some years in development. First attempts to use acoustic waves to carry electromagnetic signals explored bulk compression waves in solids, but these were difficult to tap and involved great losses. The surface wave can be produced and received easily within certain frequencies and can be tapped at any point by the simple expedient of placing a strain sensitive resistance on the surface. The waves can be coupled into other devices, split into constituent frequencies by thin layers or one tapered layer deposited on the surface, and can even be amplified by the use of a semiconductor layer under a piezoelectric surface layer.

A typical device, used for delay purposes along, consists of a small slice of a suitable crystalline material such as sapphire, with the necessary *transducers* at either end. Several types of transducer have been developed, all of them making use of the *piezoelectric effect* to turn electromagnetic oscillations into a physical oscillation. The illustration (Figure 8.1) shows three types

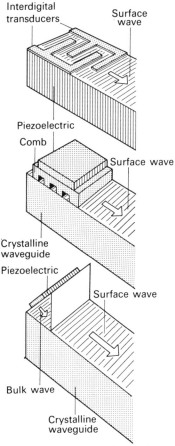

Figure 8.1 Types of acousto-electric transducer for producing surface waves.

of transducer. The first is a series of interdigital transducers on a piezo-electric substrate. The spacing of the fingers is designed so that the electromagnetic signal travelling down them progressively reinforces the surface wave set up in the piezoelectric substrate. The other two devices illustrated do not require piezoelectric waveguides and use tiny metal combs or crystalline wedges activated by piezoelectric crystals to produce the required surface pulsing on the solid. The wedge device operates by impinging a bulk compression wave on the surface of the waveguide at an angle to it. In the first two devices the frequencies that can be transmitted are limited by the mechanical spacing of the transducer 'fingers' or 'teeth'. Signals can be received at the other end of the solid waveguide by the same type of transducers (see Figure 8.2).

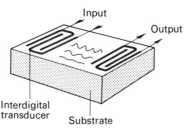

Figure 8.2   A simple delay device using interdigital transducers.

Interest in surface wave acoustics is growing rapidly, and the prospect is not simply for smaller, cheaper circuit elements. It will also be possible to perform operations on signals that are at present impossible. Signals may be read back to front, interleaved with others and processed in quite new ways.

(*From an article entitled 'New Wave in Acoustics' by Glen Lawes*, New Scientist, *vol. 44, No. 670, 9 October 1969.*)

Questions

1   Explain the meaning of the following words or phrases as used in the article:
- (a) seismology
- (b) propagates
- (c) attenuation
- (d) electromagnetic waves
- (e) transducers
- (f) piezoelectric effect

2   Indicate the unusual properties of surface waves compared with other types of wave.

3   What applications of surface waves are suggested in the article? Describe in detail how a surface wave device can be made to operate as a delay line.

4   Explain carefully the action of any one of the piezoelectric transducers described in the article.

5   Describe how a strain sensitive resistance can be used to 'tap' the surface wave at any point.

9 Segregation and sedimentation of red blood cells in ultrasonic standing waves

The formation of bands of red cells in the blood vessels of live chick embryos during *ultrasonication* has been reported by Dyson, Woodward and Pond, *Nature* 232, 572; 1971. It was suggested that the segregation was primarily caused by Bernoulli forces between the cells owing to the displacement of the cells relative to the plasma, and that the standing wave was operative only in fixing the position of the segregation pattern. Here we suggest that it is primarily the standing wave which is the cause of the segregation.

During sonication of whole blood and whole blood cultures in poly-styrene containers at intensities of about 3 W cm^{-2} at 1 MHz, the natural sedimentation of the red cells is greatly accelerated. On resuspension of the red cells, the sedimentation time in the absence of sonication returns to normal. Viscosity measurements made on the blood and the plasma during sonication show no significant change. In sonicated blood cultures, where the density of red cells is relatively low, the red cells segregate into bands at right angles to the direction of propagation of the ultrasound and with a *half wavelength periodicity* clearly related to the existence of acoustic standing waves. This effect also exists in whole blood during sonication, but is evident only when very small containers (1 mm thick) are used, as the higher density of red cells tends to mask the effect. Increased sedimentation is observed when the segregation bands are in a vertical plane. On re-orientating the sonication so that the bands are horizontal there is no apparent increase in sedimentation. This suggests that the increase in sedimentation rate is due to convection currents caused by the periodic variation of density of the cell suspensions (see Figure 9.1).

Microphone and *sensitized thermistor probe* scans within the containers show the presence of standing waves. If the hard polystyrene containers are replaced with cells made from polythene membrane about 10 μm thick, no standing wave, no increase in sedimentation rate and no segregation can be detected for intensities up to 5 W cm^{-2}. When an acoustic reflector, how-ever, is placed behind the cell (Figure 9.2) to create a standing wave, almost instantaneous segregation and rapid sedimentation occur. Moving the poly-thene cell along the axis of propagation causes the segregation to move rela-tive to the cell, but remain stationary relative to the reflector and *transducer*. It is necessary to establish a 'dose response' of red cell segregation to the magnitude of the standing wave and relate this to standing waves which might exist in the

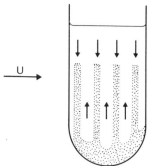

Figure 9.1 Schematic diagram of segregation and sedimentation of red blood cells. Arrows denote convection currents. U, direction of ultrasound.

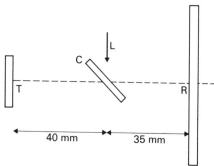

Figure 9.2 Arrangement for measuring segregation time as a function of progressive wave intensity. Reflector is removed for intensity measurement. T, transducer; C, polythene film cell; L, illuminating light beam; R, acoustic reflector.

body during clinical use of ultrasound. The segregation times determined for a range of transducer voltages for both whole blood and the 1:10 blood/plasma are shown in Figure 9.3. The abscissa shows the intensity of a plane progressive wave which, if totally reflected, would result in the segregation time shown on the ordinate. Segregation was detected by viewing the transmission of an intense focus light beam through the cell at right angles to the ultrasound propagation direction. *This criterion is arbitrary* but leads to reproducible results for segregation times. The experimental intensities were measured by a swinging ball radiation balance, Hill C. R., *Physics Med. Biol.* **15**, 241; 1970, and were *extrapolated* for intensities too low for the balance to measure. The intensities may be compared directly with those quoted for clinical use, since clinical machines are calibrated in terms of progressive wave intensity. With the exception of tissue/air interfaces, however, there is not

100 per cent reflexion from other boundaries within the body. The progressive wave intensity must be increased by a factor of $1/R$, where R is the *intensity reflexion coefficient*, to produce a standing wave of the same amplitude.

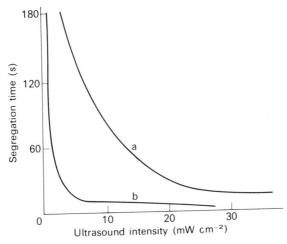

Figure 9.3 Time for visible segregation as a function of plane progressive wave intensity, for 100 per cent reflexion. a, whole blood; b, 1:10 blood/plasma.

Segregation occurs in whole blood within 30 s at intensities as low as 20 mW cm^{-2}. In 1:10 blood/plasma segregation will occur at 3 mW cm^{-2} and this figure might apply to whole blood were it not for the masking effect of the high density of red cells. These intensities are below those used clinically for foetal pulse detection and far below therapeutic intensities.

These observations raise two questions. First, what standing wave amplitudes are likely to occur in the body during clinical use of ultrasound? Second, to what extent does the segregation constitute a hazard and to what extent is it nullified by normal blood flow? Before these questions can be answered, a back absorber must be used on the opposite side of the patient from that to which the transducer is applied, to eliminate the almost 100 per cent reflexion at the body/air interface.

Work by Dyson *et al.* suggests that the red cell segregation is broken down very rapidly by normal heart action, even at high intensities. The extent to which this is so in fine capillaries must be investigated, as a barrier of high viscosity such as the segregation band would present a much higher impedance to flow. That the segregation time is reduced when the density of red cells is reduced is not consistent with the suggestion that segregation is due to Bernoulli forces. These mutually attractive forces would be diminished by increasing the average distance between the red cells and would lead to an increase in segregation time.

(From an article by N. Vashon Baker, Nature, vol. 239, No. 5372, 13 October 1972.)

Questions

1 Explain the meaning of the following words or phrases as used in the article:
   (a) ultrasonication
   (b) half wavelength periodicity
   (c) sensitized thermistor probe
   (d) transducer
   (e) this criterion is arbitrary
   (f) extrapolated
   (g) intensity reflexion coefficient

2 Describe carefully how a standing wave can be set up in a medium by reflexion of an incident progressive wave, and explain how this could lead to segregation of red blood cells from the plasma during ultrasonication of a blood sample.

3 Describe how a 'dose response' of red cell segregation was established.

4 Suggest the mechanism of operation by which a sensitized thermistor probe can detect a standing wave pattern in the blood sample.

5 Summarize the main points of the experiments which lead to the conclusion that segregation is caused, and not merely fixed, by formation of a standing wave. Mention the contribution of convection currents in the sedimentation process.

6 Discuss the earlier suggestion that segregation could be due to the operation of Bernoulli forces in the blood. Indicate the evidence which leads Baker to doubt that Bernoulli forces are primarily responsible for the effect.

7 State two specific uses of ultrasound in clinical situations and suggest the possibility of hazards arising from its use.

10 Submillimetre wave sensing of nocturnal moths

The development of insects resistant to chemical pesticides has created a strong need for optical traps to control populations of economically important insects. But first it is necessary to understand their response to electromagnetic radiation. In 1968, preliminary tests indicated that *pulsed coherent radiation* of 337 μm wavelength might be attractive to insects. We have now made a behavioural and theoretical study of this phenomenon, using the fall army worm (*Spodoptera frufiperda*), the corn earworm (*Heliothis zea*), the Indian meal moth (*Plodia interpunctella*) and the codling moth (*Carpocapsa pomonella*).

Behavioural experiments were conducted using hydrogen cyanide and water vapour lasers producing signals at wavelengths of 28, 118, 311 and 337 μm and power levels between 16 and 50 mW to evaluate the frequency dependence of response. We used male *S. frugiperda* and *H. zea*, between 12 and 72 h old. All the tests were conducted during the period of peak nocturnal activity (8.00 p.m. to 1.00 a.m., EST). The experimental set-up is illustrated in Figure 10.1. The test chamber was a plastic cylinder of ten centimetres in diameter and two metres long and most moths were at the

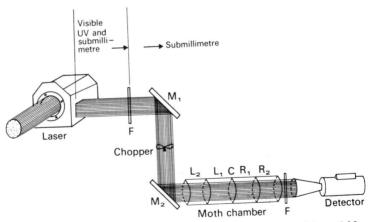

Figure 10.1 Diagram showing laser and moth test chamber. M_1 and M_2 are mirrors and F is a polyethylene filter.

end opposite the laser before the power was turned on. The number of moths attracted to the laser was counted as a function of time after the laser was switched on.

Precautions were taken to ensure that the moths responded to the sub-millimetre wave radiation and not to any other stimulant. Experiments were conducted in a darkened room (21 °C) and moths were counted using a red filtered flashlight. To reduce the visible and ultraviolet radiation emitted from the lasers, the ends of the test chamber were covered with black poly-ethylene with *zero transmission* in this region of the spectrum. The test cage was also covered with a black cloth to screen it from the visible radiation emitted from the laser plasma tube. To eliminate any doubt with regard to the test room bias the laser was detuned for 10 min and behaviour was ob-served before each experiment. (When the laser is detuned the output power drops to zero while the visible and ultraviolet radiation remain at the same level.)

A strong attraction of both species to 337 and 311 μm radiation was observed, but the response at 311 μm was less pronounced than at 337 μm (Figure 10.2). *S. frugiperda* was not attracted to 28 or 118 μm radiation.

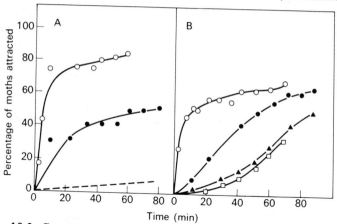

Figure 10.2 Response of male *S. frugiperda* (A) and male *H. zea* (B) to electromagnetic radiation. The radiation wavelengths are 337 μm ($\circ$),, 311 μm ($\bullet$), 118 μm ($\blacktriangle$) and 28 μm ($\square$). The dashed line is the response to incoherent BL source. *S. frugiperda* did not respond at 118 and 28 μm.

The response of male *S. frugiperda* to an attractant light (7.5 W BL lamp) in similar environmental conditions is included for comparison. *Chopping the radiation* at a rate between 600 and 3000 min^{-1} did not affect the response at 337 μm, but the attraction of *H. zea* to 118 μm increased slightly with a chopping rate of 2400 min^{-1}. Further experiments indicate that the 337 μm radiation induces changes in the activity of the moths and reduces mating potential. Exposure of both species to 337 μm (50 mW) for 0·5 h inactivated them for the rest of the night although the experiment was conducted at the beginning of the nocturnal activity period. The effect was more noticeable with *S. frugiperda*. Also, when fifteen virgin female *H. zea* were introduced in a cage containing twenty-nine male, one each 5 min (10.30 p.m. to 12.30 a.m., EST) in the presence of 16 mW at 337 μm wavelength, fourteen out of them were attracted to the laser and no mating was observed.

Looking for a theoretical basis for these responses, we conducted experiments which show the failure of incoherent infrared sources, and coherent radiation from Klystrons (0.8 to 3.5 cm) and a gallium arsenide diode (0.85 μm) to elicit the response of the moths. This indicates the absence of electromagnetic thermal detectors in the moth system and suggests that the moths respond to invisible radiation through *tuned structures*. Macroscopically the main spines of these moths' antennae are hollow thin-walled tubes with tapered cross section and periodic variation in the outside diameter. This structure is suitable as a *dielectric antenna* coupling electromagnetic radiation between the moth and its environment.

In conclusion, insects are strongly attracted to a submillimetre radiation source. Theoretical study on the moth antennae together with the frequency dependence of their response strongly suggests that the antennae may be the receptor through which insects are stimulated to respond. The response is very pronounced and has strong potential for optical traps to control the population of pest insects.

(*From an article by I. I. Eldumiati and W. C. Levengood*, Nature, vol. 233, No. 5317, 24 September 1971.)

Questions

1 Explain the meaning of the following words or phrases as used in the article:
   (a) pulsed coherent radiation
   (b) zero transmission
   (c) chopping the radiation
   (d) tuned structures
   (e) dielectric antenna

2 Describe the precautions taken to ensure that the moths were responding only to the submillimetre radiation.

3 Summarize the results of the experiments with respect to the response of the moths to the radiation.

4 What is the suggested explanation for the effect on the moths?

5 Discuss possible advantages of optical traps over conventional methods of insect control.

11   Electrostatic printing

One great advantage of electrostatic printing is that for the first time it is no longer necessary to bring the print and paper into contact, making it possible to print on some very unusual surfaces — corrugated cardboard, cotton wool or even the yolk of a raw egg.

Broadly speaking, electrostatic printing is any process in which a visible pattern is produced on paper, or other media, through the influence of an electric field. A simple experiment demonstrates the way in which one type of electrostatic printer works: a piece of dielectric-coated paper is placed over a flat sheet of metal and a length of copper wire put on top of the paper. A d.c. potential of a few hundred volts is then applied between the two conductors — the wire and the metal sheet. After the wire has been removed and the dielectric surface dusted with an insulating powder, the powder can be seen clinging to the area which the wire covered. What happens is that a layer of charge is generated on the top surface which attracts the powder particles; these in turn also become charged. The particles cling quite tenaciously and, if they are made of a *thermoplastic material*, they can be fixed permanently to the paper simply by applying heat.

Printing at 'television' speed

If a large number of separate electrodes are used instead of a single piece of wire, any desired pattern can be printed. A straightforward way of doing this would be to have separate leads to each electrode and to apply the voltage through an array of switches — one for each electrode. Quite obviously, this would need far too many wires and switches to be practicable — even for the most simple of patterns. Nevertheless, because of the phenomenal speed at which these charge patterns can be set up, *alphanumeric printers* — those using characters composed of the alphabet and the numbers nought to nine — based on this principle are making the quest for really high-speed printing a reality. At present, research has shown that legible marks can be made on paper by voltage pulses as short as 20 nanoseconds.

At the Stanford Research Institute, we have found a solution to the switching problem. An electron beam which scans across the ends of an array of wires at the target end of a cathode-ray tube is essentially a very rapid switch. When the beam strikes a particular wire, that wire begins to charge towards the cathode potential of the tube and can be brought to a voltage of several hundred volts, with respect to earth, in a fraction of a microsecond. This offers a splendid means for printing a character pattern on paper at the same speed as a picture can be produced on a television screen.

This is the underlying principle of the Videograph system manufactured by A. B. Dick Company of Chicago. One form of the Videograph is being used to print address labels for magazines at the rate of 36 labels per second. In this case the cathode-ray printing tube, which is just under three inches wide, contains *a matrix* of short, fine wires embedded in a face plate (see Figure 11.1). The addresses are stored on magnetic tape in a large computer

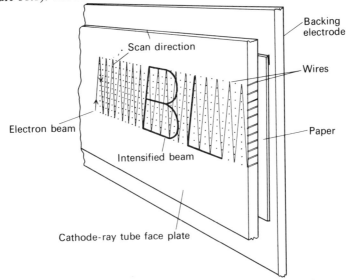

Figure 11.1 Cathode-ray tubes used in the Videograph system has a 'screen' made of a matrix of short, fine wires, and can print 50 000 characters a second.

which feeds the printer with information in digital form. Part of the printer consists of a character generator which transforms the digital code into electrical patterns that correspond to the alphanumeric characters. The generator causes the electron beam in the printing tube to scan a small region where a character is to be printed. The intensity at which it does this varies, that is to say it is *intensity modulated*, so that the beam can be turned on and off at the proper time, and the desired charge pattern produced.

The corona effect

In the demonstration experiment described above, if the top electrode – the copper wire – is discharged before it is removed from the paper, little or no charge remains on the surface and it is quite impossible to develop a satis-factory image. However, as the voltage between the base metal sheet and the electrode is raised, a threshold is eventually reached where the charge is irreversibly deposited on the paper — even when the top electrode is earthed before being taken away. The exact mechanism of this effect is not fully understood, but it appears that the charge is due to a 'corona' formation or discharge at the edges of the electrode.

Thus there are two distinct phenomena associated with depositing charges

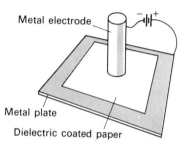

Metal electrode

Metal plate

Dielectric coated paper

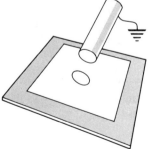

Figure 11.2   Two principles used in electrostatic printing.

from single electrodes on dielectric surfaces: the first is similar to the behaviour of a parallel plate capacitor, and the second closely resembles the discharge from the sharp edges of a high-voltage electrode. The appearance of the patterns produced by the two effects is quite different. The first effect produces a pattern which looks very much like the electrode – broad areas of contact being well exposed. In the second case, the pattern produced by, say, a flat circular electrode tends to produce a ring shape – indicating that the discharge has occurred around the well defined edges rather than over the flat surface (see Figure 11.2). A solid cylindrical electrode is connected through a battery to a flat metal plate electrode, and a piece of dielectric coated paper placed between the two (top). When the upper electrode is removed (middle) a charged pattern, the shape of the electrode, is left behind; this is made visible by dusting with a powder called 'toner'. If, however, the upper electrode is earthed before being removed (bottom), no charge remains unless the voltage has been raised above a certain 'threshold'. In this case, the pattern shows only the outline of the electrode. This 'corona' effect can be produced even when the electrode does not actually touch the paper – making possible printing on delicate surfaces.

(*From an article by Philip Rice*, Discovery, *July 1964.*)

Questions

1 Explain the meaning of the following words or phrases as used in the article:
  (a) thermoplastic material
  (b) alphanumeric printers
  (c) a matrix
  (d) intensity modulated

2 Explain the principle of the high speed switching system developed at the Stanford Research Institute.

3 Describe how this device is 'tied-in' to a computer to print addresses stored on magnetic tape.

4 What are the phenomena associated with the deposition of charge from single electrodes on dielectric surfaces? Explain how the pattern is formed in each case.

5 Give two practical instances where the corona effect would facilitate printing on delicate surfaces.

12 Thunderclouds and lightning discharge

The thundercloud

Thunderclouds have usually two main centres of charge, with the lower charge being negative, as in Figure 12.1. Both charges are of the order of 20 coulombs and are separated by a vertical distance of about 3 km. The whole cloud is between 5 and 10 km high and has a base diameter of several kilometres. A very readable account of the research work into the electrical structure of thunderclouds is contained in a book by B. J. Mason, *Clouds, Rain and Rainmaking* (Cambridge, 1962).

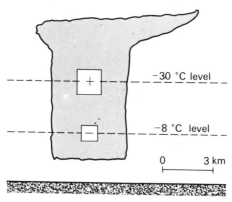

Figure 12.1   The electrical structure of a thundercloud.

Each individual thundercloud usually exists for about 30 minutes, during which time it may produce lightning flashes as often as once every 20 seconds. As each flash will destroy most of the 20 coulombs of charge, the thundercloud must be a generator of *static electricity*. 20 coulombs destroyed every 20 seconds is equivalent to an average current dissipated by lightning of about 1 ampere. Possible mechanisms for this charge separation are discussed by Mason (*op. cit.*) and J. A. Chalmers, *Atmospheric Electricity* (Pergamon, 1967). According to Mason about 66 per cent of lightning flashes are between charges in the cloud and not to earth. So the average current carried to earth by lightning in a single thunderstorm is about 0.3 ampere.

Calculation of the electric field under a thundercloud

The size of the electric field under a thunderstorm will influence both the current flowing in a lightning conductor and the possibility of a lightning flash to ground. Because the earth is a good conductor compared to air, an approximate value for this electric field can be calculated using the method of images. A negative charge Q will induce positive and negative charges into the surface of the earth as in Figure 12.2(a). It can be seen that the same pattern of *lines of force* will be obtained if the conductor did not exist and a positive charge Q was placed as in Figure 12.2(b). The actual electric field at the ground will be the same as the field halfway between these two charges.

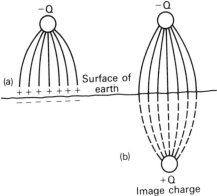

Figure 12.2   The use of the method of images to calculate the electric field below a cloud.

So the electric field E^- at the ground due to the negative charge Q, situated at height h_1 above the ground is given by:

$$E^- = -\frac{2Q}{4\pi\epsilon_0 h_1{}^2}$$

where ϵ_0 is the permittivity of free space.
The electric field due to a positive charge Q at a height h_2 is given by:

$$E^+ = \frac{2Q}{4\pi\epsilon_0 h_2{}^2}.$$

So the resultant field E due to the two main charges of a thunderstorm will be:

$$E = E^- + E^+$$
$$= \frac{Q}{2\pi\epsilon_0}\left[\frac{1}{h_2{}^2} - \frac{1}{h_1{}^2}\right].$$

Taking $Q = 20$ C, $h_2 = 6$ km and $h_1 = 3$ km, the electric field at the ground will be approximately 30 000 V m^{-1}. It must be emphasized that the actual value of the field will vary considerably from storm to storm; also many thunderclouds are thought to have a small positive charge below the main negative charge.

The lightning flash

An electric discharge will occur in dry air at atmospheric pressure in electric fields of above 3×10^6 V m^{-1}; however, the average field below the thundercloud is only of the order of 3×10^4 V m^{-1}. Several factors assist the development of a lightning stroke. In small regions within the cloud the electric field may be locally very high due to localized patches of charge. Water drops tend to become deformed in the high electric fields and *corona discharge* will start from the pointed ends. Larger drops are more easily deformed by electric fields, and if drops of several millimetres in diameter are present, electric breakdown may occur in fields as low as 5×10^5 V m^{-1}. Once the lightning stroke has started in one part of the cloud it will continue in the smaller fields below.

The complex nature of the lightning discharge has been revealed by Sir Basil Schonland using a special camera designed by C. V. Boys. A description of this technique is given by D. J. Malan, *Physics of Lightning* (English University Press, 1963). The first visible sign of the lightning discharge is the *stepped leader* in which the negative charge from the base of the cloud moves downwards in a series of steps of 10 to 200 metres in length, as in Figure 12.3. The leader stroke follows a zigzag path with the tip advancing at a speed of about 10^5 m s^{-1}. When the leader approaches within about 50 m of the ground it is met by an upward-moving streamer

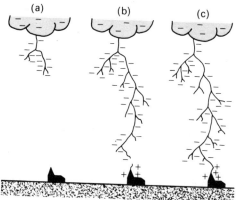

Figure 12.3 The initial stages of a lightning discharge: (a) the start of the stepped leader; (b) the positive streamer leaves the ground; (c) the positive streamer joins the stepped leader.

of positive charge. A conducting path between the cloud and the ground has now been established and the main or return stroke flows along this ionized path. The return stroke carries the main current of the discharge which is of the order of 10 amperes and which lasts for typically 100 μs. The tip of the return stroke advances at about one-tenth of the speed of light, considerably faster than the original leader stroke. If the cloud has not been fully discharged by the return stroke, further strokes along the same channel are likely to occur.

B. F. J. Schonland, *The Flight of Thunderbolts* (Clarendon, 1964), estimated the potential difference between cloud and earth immediately before a lightning flash to be typically between 10^8 and 10^9 volts. As the quantity of charge flowing to earth is about 20 coulombs, the energy released by a lightning discharge is of the order of 10^{10} joules. Mason (*op. cit.*) has estimated that 75 per cent of this energy is dissipated in heating up the air column surrounding the discharge path. This causes a rapid expansion of the air and the radiation of sound waves which are heard as thunder.

(From an article entitled 'Thunderclouds and Lightning Conductors' by P. F. Martin, The School Science Review, Vol. 54, June 1973. Used with the permission of The Association for Science Education.)

Questions

1 Explain the meaning of the following words or phrases as used in the article:
  (a) static electricity
  (b) lines of force
  (c) corona discharge
  (d) stepped leader

2 Describe the structure of a thundercloud and suggest a mechanism by which the cloud is able to generate static electricity.

3 State what factors encourage the development of a lightning stroke and summarize the steps in the chain from the formation of the first stepped leader to complete discharge of the cloud.

4 Explain the origin of the sound energy familiar to us as a thunderclap.

13 Magnetohydrodynamics

Faraday's second law states that if a conductor moves in a magnetic field, a current will flow in the conductor in a direction at right angles to both the direction of its motion and the magnetic field. There is nothing in this law which suggests that the conductor need be a solid, and indeed Lord Kelvin showed that (salty and therefore conducting) tidal water flowing in a river estuary in the Earth's magnetic field can act as a simple generator. The modern concept of an MHD generator is not fundamentally different from Kelvin's experiments, except that an electrically conducting gas flowing at high speed past the electrodes is used as the working fluid instead of water and the Earth's weak magnetic field is replaced by that of a powerful electromagnet (see Figure 13.1). In general, gases are poor electrical conductors, though their conductivity can be increased to the levels necessary for

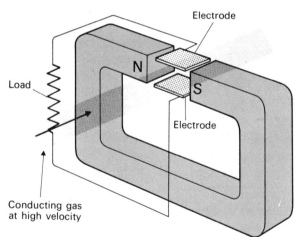

Figure 13.1 Simplified diagram showing the principle of MHD power generation.

MHD power generation by heating to, say, 3000 K and adding small concentrations of salts of metals with *low ionization potentials* – a process known as 'seeding'. On ionization, the alkali metals produce free electrons which act as current-carriers in the gas stream.

In a typical generation unit, air (or oxygen) is compressed to about 500 kN m^{-2} and preheated in *a heat exchanger* to 1700 K before passing to a combustion chamber (see Figure 13.2). The mixture of air and flue gas leaving the furnace at around 3100 K is allowed to expand through a nozzle down to a pressure of 10 kN m^{-2}, thereby attaining a very high velocity as it passes between the electrodes from which current is drawn. Gases leave the generator at around 1800 K and can be used to preheat incoming air before passing to a conventional generator unit. The system as described is of the open cycle type and has the disadvantage of venting costly and corrosive seed material to the atmosphere. Closed cycle schemes have also been investigated and these would be used where the combustion chamber was replaced by a nuclear reactor, in order to reduce radioactive hazards.

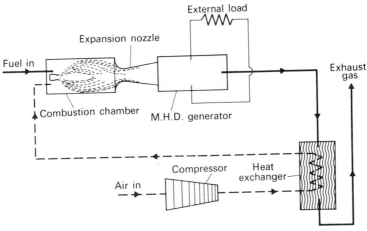

Figure 13.2   Open cycle MHD power generator.

Whilst the fundamental principles of MHD are well understood, the development of a practical generator poses enormous problems, mainly due to the lack of suitable materials capable of withstanding the very high temperatures involved. The electrodes, for example, become very hot and must therefore be made from a *refractory material*, at the same time possessing a reasonable electrical conductivity. In the design of a generator, economics is the over-riding factor. For example, the lower the gas conductivity, the larger is the duct length required for slowing down the gas and converting its kinetic energy into electrical energy. In order to build a generator of realistic length (say 10 m for a 100 MW unit) a conductivity of at least 10 A V^{-1} m^{-1} is required. This can be achieved by heating the gases in the duct to above 2300 K where thermal ionization of the seed is sufficient, though this involves the materials problem already mentioned. Other methods of attaining the required conductivity which have been investigated include the use of *shock waves* (high-velocity shock waves passed through a gas can increase the percentage of ionization to 20–30 per cent compared with the fraction of a per cent obtained by high-temperature seeding), the addition of solid particles of thermionic emitters to the gases and utilization of non-equilibrium ionization existing in certain parts of flames. For example, the addition of halogens to flames can promote abnormally high ionization at gas temperatures easily contained in conventional furnace materials.

The output of MHD generators as described is of course direct current and although this may be converted to a.c. relatively cheaply, suggestions have been made in which an oscillating shock wave or flame front passes between the electrodes, thus producing an a.c. form directly.

Materials problems have so far limited the net output (i.e. in excess of that required for the compressors and the electromagnet) of an experimental MHD generator to about 10 kW (for any length of time), though in view of the development work on new materials and techniques by which high gas conductivities are achieved at lower temperatures carried out at present, it seems reasonable to expect that a practical and efficient MHD production unit will emerge in the not-too-distant future.

(*From an article entitled 'Energy Conversion' by J. H. Harker*, School Science Review, *Vol. 51, March 1970. Used with the permission of The Association for Science Education.*)

Questions

1 Explain the meaning of the following words or phrases as used in the article:
  (a) low ionization potentials
  (b) a heat exchanger
  (c) a refractory material
  (d) shock waves

2 A tidal river estuary (salty and therefore conducting) has straight, parallel banks and the water is flowing due east in a region where the horizontal component of the earth's magnetic field has a flux density of 2×10^{-5} T and the angle of dip is $70°$. If the average speed of flow is 15 km h^{-1} estimate the potential difference which exists between two points 500 m apart in a horizontal line perpendicular to the direction of flow.

3 How does seeding increase the conductivity of the working gas in an MHD generator?

4 Describe briefly the mode of operation of a typical MHD generation unit.

5 What are the problems associated with a practical MHD unit?

6 Summarize the methods available for increasing the gas conductivity and explain carefully how an a.c. output can be achieved.

14 Transport of excitons

When light in the visible or ultraviolet part of the spectrum is absorbed in a solid, the photon is converted into an excitation of the atoms. It is a very important feature of some electronic excitations that they can be transferred very efficiently from atom to atom and that energy can thus be transported away from an illuminated surface. Such processes are important in fields as diverse as power generation, photography and biosynthesis. Although these concepts of energy transfer can be elaborated theoretically, it is not at all easy to detect this transfer and identify the mode precisely. In the absorption spectrum of a semiconductor or dielectric, one of the most intense absorptions is at an energy slightly less than that of the *forbidden energy gap*. The theory is that a photon at this energy is converted into an excited pair consisting of an electron and a hole. The electron and the hole do not drift apart but stay bound to each other. They are not, however, too tightly bound to the parent atom. They represent packets of energy which can, in theory, drift through the network of atoms by means of a very efficient quantum mechanical transfer or 'resonant transfer' of energy (Dexter and Knox, *Excitons*, Wiley; 1969). The importance of the exciton configuration is the high level of stored energy (say 6 eV for an alkali halide) and the theoretically long time before recombination.

Although the lifetime of an exciton is expected to be long in an ideal solid lattice, it may be limited to a few nanoseconds in a typical real solid by surfaces and lattice defects; a typical diffusion range is much less than a millimetre. It is, however, difficult to find where an exciton started its life and where it was annihilated. No current flows and no track is left. One is obliged to try to observe the effects of the energy released at annihilation and to eliminate the possibility of other forms of energy transport from the region where the light was absorbed. Several attempts have been made to measure the exciton diffusion length in cadmium sulphide. For example, Broser and Balkanski (Z. *Elektrochem.*, 61, 715; 1957) illuminated a crystal with a fine spot of light and found that this could produce an electric current between two electrodes in a different region. The migration of energy could, however, possibly be accounted for by absorption and re-emission of light. Another important energy transfer process involving excitons was proposed in a satisfying new model for the formation of *F-centres* in alkali halides (Pooley, *Proc. Phys. Soc.*, 87, 245, 257; 1966; Hersh, *Phys. Rev.* 148, 928; 1966).

In this model, kinetic energy from an exciton annihilation is used to start a focused collision sequence in a crystal which ends with the expulsion of a halogen atom into an interstitial site. Townsend (*Phys. Lett.* **28A**, 587; 1969) elegantly confirmed that ion motion is indeed involved when he showed that illuminating a very clean crystal of potassium iodide with light in the first exciton band could produce efficient *sputtering*. An elaboration of these experiments has now unexpectedly produced an observation which could be interpreted as exciton motion; the method has more elegance and is probably less ambiguous than earlier experiments.

Al-Jammal, Pooley and Townsend (*J. Phys. C.*, **6**, 247; 1973) recently found that an electron beam of energy of several hundred electron volts gave a surprisingly high sputtering yield in potassium iodide, with an unexpected maximum in the curve of efficiency against energy occurring at 400 eV. This result implies that energy is being transported efficiently to the surface through 25 nm of crystal (the stopping range for 400 eV electrons). Most probably the transport is excitonic. The efficiency is so high that *fluorescence* and reabsorption are unlikely. Focused collision sequences are again known to be much too inefficient; for example, if 5 eV of kinetic energy is imparted to one atom, at least 1 eV is lost in transferring that energy to the next atom and so on down a chain of atoms. Five stages of transfer would be completed within only 5 nm. Alternatively, *interstitial atom diffusion* is possible but the effects of thallium ion doping are stronger than would be expected according to this explanation. Thus one is left with exciton diffusion as the most likely mechanism.

Using some approximations to estimate the profile of electron energy deposition, Al-Jammal *et al.* estimate the exciton diffusion length to be about 20 nm. Probabilities of resonance transfer in KI are such that an exciton should jump every 10^{-12} s on average. For three-dimensional diffusion, the estimated typical range, 20 nm, will be achieved if the exciton lifetime is 2×10^{-8} s. This is of the same order of magnitude as the lifetime estimated by Collins (*J. Appl. Phys.* **30**, 1135; 1959) and Bleil and Broser (*J. Phys. Chem. Solids*, **25**, 11; 1964) for excitons in cadmium sulphide. Thus a fairly consistent picture emerges. It has been shown that defects serve as traps and recombination centres for excitons in many materials. Thallium in potassium iodide acts in this way and was used in this experiment to check the consistency of the exciton diffusion model. Measurements on a crystal doped with thallium showed a reduced diffusion length of only 13 nm. This result gives a *trapping cross-section* for the thallium ion which fits well with its ionic radius.

The novelty of the approach derives from the use of a surface phenomenon, namely sputtering, to measure energy release in the lattice, rather than fluorescence, which was used in most of the previous experiments.

(Nature, *Vol. 242, No. 5396, 30 March 1973.*)

Questions

1 Explain the meaning of the following words or phrases as used in the article:
  (a) forbidden energy gap
  (b) F-centres
  (c) sputtering
  (d) fluorescence
  (e) interstitial atom diffusion
  (f) trapping cross-section

2 Describe the action by which an exciton is formed and contrast its properties with those of a 'normal' electron hole pair in a semiconductor or dielectric.

3 State and discuss the factors which limit the lifetime and range of an exciton in a solid.

4 Why does the motion of an exciton cause no flow of current nor leave a track?

5 Summarize carefully the experiments which suggest transport of excitons to be a mode of energy transfer which cannot be explained by other mechanisms.

6 State, with reasons, how you would expect the following conditions to influence the behaviour of excitons:
  (a) an electric field of increasing strength
  (b) a magnetic field of increasing strength
  (c) an increase of temperature.

15   Doping solids with ions

Ion implantation is the technique of modifying the properties and composition of solids by embedding into them accelerated charged particles. The
technique is now becoming increasingly important in making semiconductors, whose electrical properties are dominated by certain impurities (*'dopants'*
in concentrations sometimes as low as one part in 10^8. These impurities are
normally introduced by *diffusion* at high temperatures but it is now clear
that ion implantation, used as a complementary processs, offers several
advantages. It is more versatile and controllable. It also gives new degrees of
freedom to the microelectronics circuit designer. Already, equipment is in
operation which allows ion implantation to be carried out cheaply and
rapidly in apparatus that is both compact and safe for industrial use.

The principal advantage of ion implantation is that it is a relatively low-
temperature process in which the depth and uniformity of doping in the
solid can be precisely controlled. Particles enter the solid as a directed beam
with little or no sideways deflection. Thus, in contrast to diffusion, the
doped areas can be closely defined. Since it is not a thermal equilibrium
process, the choice of dopants is no longer limited by diffusion kinetics or
even solubility limits.

To understand how ion implantation is compatible with, and can even
exploit the conventional transistor-manufacturing techniques we must first
briefly discuss the standard method of making planar semiconductor devices.
The starting point of the process is normally a thin wafer of high purity,
single-crystal silicon one or two inches in diameter. A layer of silicon oxide
is grown or deposited on the surface. Precise patterns of regularly-spaced,
minute windows are etched through the oxide by an ingenious photolitho-
graphic process. The slice is then heated in a furnace containing the vapour
of the required dopant, which diffuses into the silicon surface only in those
areas where the windows have been opened. The process of oxidation, etching
and diffusion can be repeated until the final complex, layered structure is
obtained. A suitable metal can then be evaporated over the surface and a
similar etching process carried out to make the electrical contacts and inter-
connections. The finished slice may be cut into more than 100 identical chips,
each containing a complete electrical circuit of many transistors.

Now to the ion doping. It may eventually be possible to 'write' the desired
doping pattern directly on to the slice with a focused-spot ion beam. But at

present the surface of the slice is masked in the same way during ion bombardment as in the diffusion process, and the whole surface of the slice is then uniformly bombarded with ions. Ions penetrate the semiconductor only through the opened windows. Because of the directional nature of the accelerated ion beam, the edges of the mask precisely define the area of the doped regions. In diffusion, on the other hand, there is considerable sideways spread under the mask. This important advantage of implantation has led to significant improvements in the performance of metal-oxide semiconductor transistors (MOSTs).

The ion implantation equipment is relatively modest by nuclear accelerator standards. Although some research has been carried out with ions with energies of the order of millions of electron volts, it is now generally accepted that much lower energies are normally sufficient. The majority of studies are, in fact, carried out at below 150 keV. Under these conditions small and relatively simple accelerators can be used.

For reproducible results, it is essential to minimize hydrocarbon contamination of the surface (e.g. by pump oil), otherwise a *tenacious film* of carbon builds up. Likewise, dust must be scrupulously eliminated. Even small particles will shadow the underlying semiconductor, presenting an even more serious problem than in the case of diffusion. After bombardment the specimens must be *annealed*: here, however, the temperatures are much lower than the 1000 °C or more that is typical of diffusion. 650 °C is sufficient to restore silicon after most ion bombardments, and the electrical behaviour is then controlled by the chemical nature of the dopant. Alternatively, the specimen may be implanted while hot, at say 450 °C in the case of silicon. Under such conditions the radiation damage anneals out rapidly during bombardment.

Let us now examine specific devices which can be made with advantage using ion implantation. In avalanche photo-diodes and nuclear radiation detectors it is important to have a *uniform junction* that can withstand high reverse voltages. The enhanced diffusion which tends to occur along defects in the crystal leads to a *spiky junction* and localized breakdown. Ion implantation eliminates this and has produced excellent diodes in both silicon and germanium. Several workers have reported device yields superior to those obtained by other techniques. Ion implantation, with its close control over ion penetration, has been used to produce shallow junctions in solar cells and nuclear particle detectors. It should also have virtues in the production of high-frequency oscillator devices.

In *bi-polar transistors* (the commonest variety of transistor in use today), implantation greatly reduces the 'push-out' effect, by which the strain introduced during diffusion of one electrode causes an undesirable movement of a previously introduced junction. If the second stage is carried out by implantation, the inter-electrode spacing (base width) of the transistor can be reduced to 100 to 200 nm. Other things being equal, a better high-frequency performance should thus be achievable than in a diffused device.

More striking improvements have been obtained with MOSTs. These transistors are becoming increasingly important, notably in integrated circuit arrays where their low power consumption is valuable. A drawback to making them by conventional diffusion is the uncontrolled spreading of the dopant under the oxide layer (see Figure 15.1). This leads to an overlap of the

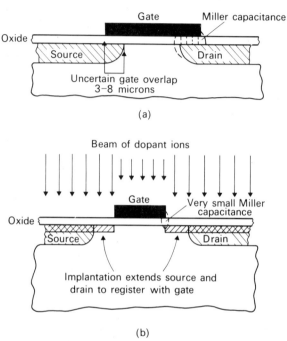

(a)

(b)

Figure 15.1 Diagrammatic cross-sections of conventional (a) and ion-implanted (b) metal-oxide semiconductor transistors (MOSTs), illustrating the technique for minimizing inter-electrode capacitance by using ion-implantation. In this type of transistor the flow of electrons or holes between the source and the drain is controlled by a voltage applied to the gate electrode.   (Based upon work at Mullard Research Laboratories and AERE, Harwell).

various electrodes, and the resulting *parasitic capacitances* limit the performance at high frequencies and in arrays. Impurities injected by ion implantation, however, enter the semiconductor as a directed beam with essentially no lateral spreading. This can reduce the inter-electrode capacitances by a factor of 20, and considerably improve high-frequency performance. It also allows smaller, and consequently faster, transistors to be made. Such improvements in integrated circuit parameters are important in fast switching arrays.

Already, the trend towards large-scale integrated circuits, with many hundreds of component transistors on a single chip of silicon 2.5 mm square is having an impact on the cost, weight and size of electronic equipment comparable with that of the original introduction of transistors. The circuit complexity which can be achieved in practice is limited by the overall yield of the manufacturing process. The reproducibility and low temperature nature of ion implantation may well lead to better device yields. Diffusion, however, is not always the critical stage in device manufacture. There are technological problems in reproducibly making good oxide layers, in contacting semi-conductors, etc. So it may take some time before the full merits of ion implantation can be realized in the complex fabrication process.

(From an article entitled 'Doping Solids with Ions' by Geoff Dearnley and J. Harry Freeman, New Scientist, Vol. 41, No. 635, 6 February 1969.)

Questions

1 Explain the meaning of the following words or phrases as used in the article:
   (a) dopants
   (b) diffusion
   (c) tenacious film
   (d) annealed
   (e) uniform junction
   (f) spiky junction
   (g) bipolar transistors
   (h) parasitic capacitances

2 Describe briefly in your own words the techniques of diffusion and ion implantation of dopants.

3 What are the advantages of ion implantation in terms of the ease of manufacture of semiconductor devices?

4 What general improvements does this lead to in the properties and types of device available?

5 Explain, with reference to MOSTs (see Figure 15.1), the improvement in operation that is achieved by ion implantation.

6 With the aid of energy-band diagrams, describe how the addition of impurities can modify the properties of intrinsic semiconductors. Consider both n-type and p-type semiconductors and give examples in each case of a suitable dopant.

16   A rival to the transistor

The idea of a semiconducting device with an *amorphous material*, or glass, as its 'heart' is relatively new. There has recently been considerable interest in switching devices of this kind, in which the 'switch' is from a state of high electrical resistance to a state of low resistance, or the other way round, the switch taking place at a given applied voltage. Several laboratories have been working on such devices but S. R. Ovshinsky of Energy Conversion Devices Inc., Troy, Michigan, was the first to publish details of the new device in *Physical Review Letters* (Vol. 21, p. 1450).

Glasses are unlike other materials. They are not crystalline solids but are more like extremely viscous *super-cooled liquids*. In a crystal the atoms are held in a very rigid and definite geometrical relation with all the other atoms of the crystal. In a glass there exists considerable short-range (nearest neighbour) order but very little, if any, long-range order. That is, an atom may see its nearest neighbours in approximately the same positions as they would have in a crystal, but beyond these the positions of other atoms bear little resemblance to those in a single crystal. This structure difference is important in explaining the difference in electrical behaviour of glasses.

Quantum theory predicts that in a crystal, as a result of the regular periodic arrangement of atoms, an electron as described by a wave will have a definite wavelength and move a long distance before it is scattered. In glasses, due to their liquid-like or random structure, this is not so, and at best the electron moves from atom to atom being scattered each time. Moreover, there will exist a high density of localized states or 'traps' in which the electron cannot move unless supplied with extra energy.

A crystalline semiconductor has certain energy states which an electron is allowed to occupy. These, principally the valence band and conduction band — separated by a *'forbidden gap'* — are all well defined in energy. This energy picture may also be applied to glasses — but with modifications. The short-range order in a glass gives rise to the conventional bands, but because of the lack of long-range order and the presence of localized states these bands are much less clearly defined in energy. On going from a crystalline to a disordered structure, the energy states at the edge of the permitted bands enter the forbidden gap and become localized. The more these states are shifted, the greater the localization. This migration of states into the forbidden gap smears out the band edges so that they are no longer well defined. According to Professor Sir Nevill Mott of the Cavendish Laboratory, in a disordered system there exists a critical energy at which all states are non-localized and extend through the lattice. The density of localized states decreases exponentially into the forbidden gap from this critical energy edge. This brings us to the point where we may turn to the practical advantages offered by glasses in semiconductor devices. In a crystalline semiconductor, the conductivity is dependent upon the perfection of the crystal and can be varied by adding impurities. These impurities, or dopants, reside in levels within the forbidden gap, and determine not only the magnitude of the conductivity but also whether the conduction is by electrons or holes, that is, n-type or p-type respectively. The concentration of these impurities needs to be very precisely controlled, better than one part per million. Also, since the properties of a crystalline array are dependent on an ordered lattice, they are very susceptible to ionizing radiation which would disrupt the periodic array.

The *resistivity* of glasses is determined by the constituents of the 'glassy' compound and may range from one ohm metre to 10^{18} ohm metres. The addition of a small amount of impurities (up to a few per cent) has little effect on the conductivity, partly because of the presence of localized states in the forbidden gap, and partly because in a glass all available electrons are likely to be taken up in bonds. Similarly, due to the inherent disorder, radiation damage has little effect on the electrical properties of glasses.

In a switch of the type announced by Energy Conversion, fabrication is very simple compared with conventional semiconductors. It consists of a thin film of the glass between two electrodes. The device can be either of the form of two wires embedded in a glass bead and separated by a distance of a few micrometres, or as an evaporated – or 'sputtered' – sandwich configuration consisting of an evaporated metal film, then the glass film, and finally another metal film as the top electrode. The electrodes are generally metal, but may be some other material such as graphite. The glasses can also be of different kinds – for instance, the Ovshinsky device uses a glass containing tellurium, arsenic, silicon and germanium, while at the Cavendish Laboratory switching has been observed in amorphous arsenic triselenide.

The phenomenon of switching can be described by the current–voltage characteristics of a device. Take the bistable or memory switch now available from Energy Conversion. As the voltage across the device is increased from zero, the current also increases slowly in an *ohmic fashion* up to a threshold voltage, V_T. Up to this stage the device has a high resistance of the order of megohms. Once V_T is exceeded the resistance drops extremely rapidly to just a few ohms. The former is termed the high resistance or 'off' state, and the latter, the low resistance or 'on' state – hence the name 'switch'.

Once the bistable switch is in the on state the voltage may be removed and re-applied without changing the state, while the device may be switched back to the off state by a high voltage, high current pulse. The device therefore has the ability to function as a memory element for *binary notation* with the advantage of being capable of interrogation without destroying the existing memory state. This property is not exhibited by any present computer memory element. The ease of fabrication, very small size, low power-consumption, fast switching speeds, and unique memory properties promise an interesting future for these bistable switches in computer memories and other applications demanding a memory state.

The other switch, the astable switch – such as the Ovonic threshold switch – has similar high and low *impedance* states. As the applied voltage is increased up to V_T the device is in the off state; once V_T is exceeded, it switches to the on state in less than 1.5×10^{-10} second. As the current is reduced below a characteristic value termed the holding current the device switches back to the off or high impedance state. There is no memory state in the astable switch since it switches back to the high impedance state before the voltage can be reduced to zero.

The astable switch will find use in computer logic circuitry where fast switching is essential, in trigger circuits, as transient voltage and arc suppressors, and as staircase and other waveform generators. Other applications are being intensively investigated for military uses. One promising potential use is to provide an economic way to switch hundreds of thousands of individual electroluminescent elements in visual displays – such as a flat screen display for television that could conceivably be hung on the wall like a picture.

One of the important distinctions between these devices and conventional crystalline devices is that they are symmetric. The conventional devices must be operated on d.c. and the correct polarity is essential. The amorphous devices are symmetrical and exhibit the same properties regardless of the direction of the current flow. As a result, they may be operated from either a.c. or d.c., further enhancing their uniqueness as circuit elements.

(*From an article by Dr Robert F. Shaw,* New Scientist, *Vol. 40, No. 624, 21 November 1968.*)

Questions

1   Explain the meaning of the following words or phrases as used in the article:
(a)   amorphous material
(b)   super-cooled liquids
(c)   forbidden gap
(d)   resistivity
(e)   ohmic fashion
(f)   binary notation
(g)   impedance

2 Briefly compare and contrast the electron energy states in a glass and a conventional semiconductor.

3 Sketch labelled diagrams of the two physical configurations of the Ovshinsky switch.

4 Sketch the current–voltage characteristics for the bistable Ovshinsky switch.

5 Explain carefully the difference between the mode of operation of a bistable and an astable Ovshinsky switch.

6 In what sense can the bistable switch operate as a memory element; and why is it superior to conventional computer memory elements?

7 Explain why an astable switch is unable to operate as a memory element and suggest briefly how it would operate in one of the devices mentioned in the article.

17 Ultrasonic generation

Beyond the limits of human hearing — at frequencies above about 16 000 Hz, or six octaves above Middle C — lies the range of ultrasonic waves. Not surprisingly, the generation and use of these very high frequency 'sound' waves has stimulated the imagination of physicists and engineers for many years. For as the pioneer work on high power ultrasonic energy showed, as far back as the 1930s, this range of the sound spectrum has very great potentialities.

The major factor contributing to increasingly rapid development in this field has been the work carried out on *transducers*, the means by which energy of various forms is converted to high frequency acoustic waves.

In all cases an ultrasonic generator consists of two fundamental components: the transducer and a suitable power supply to provide the transducer with input energy. This power source can be a compressor or pump in the case of jet transducers, or it can be electrical, supplying a *sinusoidal voltage* at the required frequency. In all cases the power supply is secondary and many alternatives are possible with any given type of transducer. Efficiency in operation lies almost wholly in the design and application of the transducer. It is possible to divide transducers into distinct types according to the method of energy conversion employed and progress has been made on improvements in all groups. Although many methods of energy conversion are available, commercial exploitation has been mainly restricted to piezoelectric, magnetostrictive and jet generators.

Piezoelectric transducers

When certain crystals with an appropriate lack of symmetry in their structure have electrical stresses applied to them in predetermined directions, they distort in shape (see Figure 17.1). Alternatively, if the crystals are mechanically disorted in the same direction an electrical potential is generated. When the sign of the applied voltage is reversed there is a corresponding change in the polarity of the mechanical movement. Thus, an alternating voltage applied to the piezoelectric material will cause a periodic vibration corresponding to the applied frequency. The amplitude of vibration is materially increased *by operating at resonance*. At the mechanical resonant frequency of the transducer the stress will be at a maximum and the proportionate

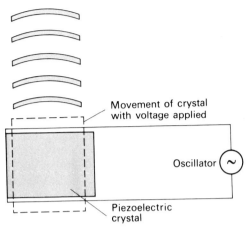

Figure 17.1 Piezoelectric transducer.

input power will be minimum. Until about 1948 all piezoelectric transducers were manufactured from single crystals of materials such as quartz and Rochelle salt.

It was originally thought that the piezoelectric effect could not be exhibited by any material unless in a single crystal form. This was proved to be wrong when polycrystalline barium titanate was shown to be strongly piezoelectric after certain initial treatments. It is in this field of polycrystalline piezoelectric ceramics that the major progress in ultrasonic transducers has been made and most of the new applications for ultrasonics use them. The property of barium titanate and similar classes of materials that influence this effect is ferroelectricity. This is the ability of certain crystals of electrically polar structure to switch the direction of polarity under the influence of a strong electrical field and to retain their new orientation after removal of the external field. The term 'ferroelectricity' is used as the effect is analogous to that shown by permanent magnetic materials, where the external influencing field is magnetic rather than electrostatic.

A piezoelectric ceramic consists of a large number of piezoelectric crystallite centres in essentially random orientation. A high electric field of between 20 to 40 kilovolts per centimetre of thickness applied to the ceramic by means of conducting electrodes will cause a preferential alignment of the crystal domains in the direction of the applied field. After polarizing, the material is piezoelectrically responsive, behaving as a single crystal.

Recent developments have shown that barium titanate is not unique in this property. Lead zirconate-titanate and niobate compounds also exhibit piezoelectric effects after polarization, the former already replacing barium titanate in many applications.

The advantages of piezoelectric ceramics over single crystal materials are obvious. They can be moulded into any required shape and then preferentially polarized to suit the mode of operation. There is no restriction on size and little wastage of raw material. The ceramic is mechanically strong and chemically inert. Electrically, the low impedance enables drive voltages to be moderate in value and insulation problems are considerably lessened.

Magnetostrictive transducers

A class of metals and semi-metals known as 'ferromagnetics' show a change in physical dimensions when subjected to a magnetic field. This is known as the magnetostriction effect and a number of ferromagnetic materials such as nickel and cobalt are capable of quite large alterations in dimension.

The process is somewhat similar to that found in a ferroelectric ceramic, but in this case the domains of magnetic moment move in an external magnetic field, producing an overall change in the dimensions of the material. It is necessary to introduce a *biasing magnetic field* and this is usually done by incorporating a permanent magnet in the magnetic circuit or by electrically inducing a magnetic field by a direct current winding. Energizing a magnetostriction transducer is carried out by supplying a winding with a sinusoidal voltage with a frequency corresponding to the resonant frequency of the mechanical system (see Figure 17.2).

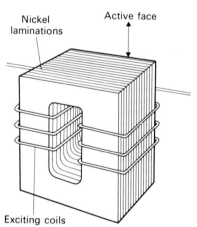

Nickel laminations

Active face

Exciting coils

Figure 17.2   Magnetostrictive transducer.

While not so adaptable and economical as a piezoelectric ceramic transducer the robust nature of the magnetostrictor and its ability to handle high powers has made them widely used for certain industrial ultrasonic applications such as drilling, soldering and welding.

The introduction of magnetostrictive ferrites, now known as piezomagnetic materials, has recently stimulated renewed interest in this type of transducer. These materials are non-metallic sinters of mixed crystals, mainly manganese, nickel and zinc oxides, and are more of a ceramic than a metal. In most cases they act as an insulator and *eddy current losses* are small due to the small crystal centres.

Depletion layer transducer

An entirely new method of transducer construction based on semiconductor techniques was described in the *Bell Laboratories Record*, 146 (April 1961). This device (see Figure 17.3) consists of a plate of semiconductor material

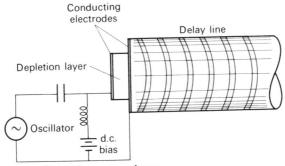

Figure 17.3 Depletion layer transducer.

such as gallium arsenide that also possesses piezoelectric properties. A thin metal film is deposited on one surface and this film acts as a *non-ohmic rectifying contact* which produces a depletion layer in the semiconductor. A depletion layer is a thin region of high resitivity formed at the interface of two dissimilar materials. The difference in certain energy levels in the two adjacent materials produces an internal electric field, which depletes the thin interface region free of mobile charge carriers, thereby decreasing its resistance. The thickness of the depletion layer can be controlled by a bias voltage across the interface. When an alternating voltage is applied, most of the voltage drop occurs across the depletion layer and it behaves like a very thin piezoelectric crystal that has been bonded to a solid bar. Since the layer is very thin the frequency is high, 1000 MHz or higher, and the large electrical field produces a very high piezoelectric stress. Since the bias voltage decides the thickness of the layer it is possible to alter the resonant frequency by voltage variation. The main use for this type of transducer is for *ultrasonic delay lines* and in laboratory studies of the acoustic properties of materials.

With the advent of new transducer principles there has been a consolidation and improvement of existing applications as well as entirely new developments in measurement, control and processing.

(From an article by Alan Crawford, Discovery, Vol. 23, September 1962.)

Questions

1   Explain the meaning of the following words or phrases as used in the article:
  (a)   transducers
  (b)   a sinusoidal voltage
  (c)   by operating at resonance
  (d)   a biasing magnetic field
  (e)   eddy current losses
  (f)   a non-ohmic rectifying contact
  (g)   ultrasonic delay lines

2   Give a summary of the characteristic properties of sound waves.

3   The article states that a frequency of 16 000 Hz is six octaves above Middle C. Taking Middle C as 261.2 Hz, show that this is true.

4   Explain what is meant by the 'piezoelectric effect' and describe how a single piezoelectric crystal can be made to generate ultrasound.

5   Describe how a polycrystalline ferrite can be polarized so as to be piezoelectrically responsive.

6   Compare the mechanism of the magnetostrictive effect with the piezoelectric effect.

7   What are the relative advantages and disadvantages of piezoelectric and piezomagnetic transducers?

8   Explain how semiconductor techniques enable the production of extremely high ultrasonic frequencies.

9   Write short notes on the uses of ultrasound in the following fields:
  (a)   industry (in its widest sense)
  (b)   medicine.

18 Industrial applications of lasers

The difference between laser or 'coherent' light and incoherent light such as is obtained from ordinary light sources is similar to the difference between electrical noise and a sinusoidal signal. It goes without saying that electronic techniques would be in a very primitive state if the only sources available were noise sources, and yet this was just the case with optical electronics before the laser appeared. Before anything like the same developments can take place at optical frequencies, as we have come to take for granted at lower frequencies, we must learn to use the new devices and to develop optical components and systems, and significant progress is being made in this direction.

The properties of laser light which make it potentially so useful are simple and obvious. First, it can be collimated to a degree limited only by diffraction, whereby the half-angle of spread θ in a system of aperture D is related to the wavelength λ by $\theta \simeq \lambda/D$. Thus, for a helium-neon laser beam of diameter 3 mm, we have $\theta \simeq 0.2$ mrad, and a simple and cheap light pencil can be produced, which has already found scores of uses in many diverse fields. For example, it is now standard equipment on tunnel-boring machines which can be programmed to keep themselves aligned on the beam, thus obviating tedious and time-consuming surveying techniques. It is used by the Boeing Aircraft Co. to line up the jig for the wing structure in the manufacture of the Jumbo jet with the result that a task which formerly took 12 h can now be done in 20 min. Somewhat unexpectedly a large volume of sales of helium-neon lasers go to night clubs and discotheques where the bright red beam is shone over walls and ceiling in synchronism with the music to produce the appropriate psychedelic effect! The application of this simple and cheap laser has been unspectacular but widespread.

As well as being collimated, a coherent beam can be focused by a lens of focal length f to a spot of diameter $d \simeq f\lambda/D$. Thus, if $f = D$, then $d \simeq \lambda$, and power densities can be achieved which are capable of melting and vaporizing any known material, and a wide range of welding, drilling and machining operations are possible. Obviously, common metals are more easily and cheaply worked by conventional techniques, but where these fail, such as with refractory or brittle materials, or where precision, purity and minimum effect on surrounding areas are of prime importance, laser machining offers a potential solution. In fact some of the first applications of lasers were, on the one hand, to the drilling of diamond dies for wire drawing resulting in a great saving in time and hence cost, and on the other hand to welding of detached retinas in eye surgery with considerable lessening of discomfort to the patient and improvement in accuracy.

With the greatly increasing complexity of microcircuits and the need for more complex designs with closer tolerances, the speed and accuracy of laser machining are becoming more widely appreciated. This facility can be used either in direct machining of the microcircuit itself or in the automatic production of primary patterns for the masks used in their preparation. Thus at Bell Telephone Laboratories, a scanning-laser-beam technique enables complex masks to be cut in 10 min that would require four days by earlier methods. Computer control of the process provides the required flexibility and speed of operation. Direct machining of thin- and thick-film circuits will also become more commercially attractive with increasing circuit complexity.

Another important property of coherent light is the ability to produce stable interference patterns which can be used in several ways. If a laser beam is split into two components which are reflected from different mirrors and recombined, the position of the peaks of the resulting pattern can be noted on a detector. Movement of one of the mirrors by a distance of half a wavelength produces a pulse in the output from the detector and a simple pulse counter gives the displacement of the mirror, and hence of the object on which it is mounted, to an accuracy of within 0·3 μm with a helium-neon laser. In fact a commercial equipment is available which has *a resolution of 10 nm*, and an accuracy within 5 parts in 10^7 and measures distances of from 0 to 60 m. It is sufficiently rugged to be used under machine-shop conditions. Systems of this kind are used in calibration of numerically controlled machine tools and co-ordinate-measuring machines and tables for such uses as precision control of microcircuit masks and substrates. Accurate long-term measurements of the movement of land masses for research and for earthquake prediction are also being made.

Another consequence of interference has given rise to *holography*, and while the ability to produce truly 3-dimensional images has not yet been widely used, the technique can record deflections of stationary or high-speed surfaces with about 1 μm resolution. Considerable effort is being directed, at the present time, to the construction of holographic stores for computers. Because a laser beam can be focused to a spot of about 1 μm diameter, one can envisage the recording of information in the form of ones and zeros as spots and lack of spots on a photographic plate. Unfortunately, this type of store would be severely affected by dust, scratches, shrinkage etc. On the other hand, in holographic recording the information is spread in the form of an interference pattern over the whole of the photographic plate and is thus almost immune to imperfections.

A hologram of a few square millimetres area can store about 10^4 bits of information, and thus an array of 100 x 100 such holograms can retain 10^8

bits. Each hologram, when addressed by a laser beam, can be so oriented as to display the image of its spot pattern on a photo-diode array. Integrated-circuit processing of the photo-diodes and high-speed deflection of the laser beam result in an access time of about 1 μs, and the cost of this random-access semipermanent page store is expected to be less than 0.01 p/bit. Other storage media are also under study in the hope that *an addressable memory* can be achieved, but it seems likely that a *megabit, microsecond store* of this type will provide an acceptable compromise between fast but expensive magnetic or semiconductor stores and cheap but slow tape stores.

Lasers have not had the widespread spectacular impact which was over-optimistically expected of them in the early 1960s, but they are being increasingly used as individual tools in a wide range of applications. However, in addition to the use of the laser as a tool, we are also witnessing the development of optical systems based on laser techniques, in keeping with the inevitable trend in electronics to ever-higher frequencies, speeds and band-widths. At present, optical systems tend to be large but, in addition to *fibre-optical waveguides*, appreciable progress has been made in optical integrated-circuit techniques, and already thin-film optical waveguides, *modulators* and couplers have been produced. With the steady improvement in stability and ruggedness of laser devices, the range of industrial applications will continue to increase, and the miniaturization of components will introduce the era of optical electronics.

(From an article entitled 'Industrial Applications of Lasers' by Prof. W. A. Gambling, Electronics and Power, Vol. 18, February 1972. Used with the permission of The Institution of Electrical Engineers.)

Questions

1 Explain the meaning of the following words or phrases as used in the article:
   (a) a resolution of 10 nm
   (b) holography
   (c) an addressable memory
   (d) a megabit, microsecond store
   (e) fibre-optical waveguides
   (f) modulators

2 What are the characteristic properties of coherent light?

3 What is the difference between electrical noise and a sinusoidal signal?

4 Name the property of laser light which enables it to be used as a 'light rule'. Give examples of applications based on this.

5   Describe instances in which the properties of lasers have led to improvements in techniques for the working of metals and other materials.

6   Explain in some detail the way in which a laser interference method can be used for the accurate determination of distances. Mention some applications of this ability to make precise measurements.

7   Discuss the possibilities of a holographic method for the storage and retrieval of information.

Part Two: Data Analysis

Hints for answering Data Analysis Papers

In the data analysis questions you will be presented with a set of raw data which will often have to be manipulated prior to plotting a graph or substituting into equations. Where a graphical analysis is required it will often be linear so that you can deduce or verify relationships between experimentally measured quantities.

Any straight line can be represented by the equation $y = mx + c$, where m is the gradient of the line plotted with y as ordinate and x as abscissa. c is the value of the intercept on the y-axis (i.e. the value of y when $x = 0$).

First rearrange the theoretical equation in linear form so that the quantities to be plotted may be determined. These should then be tabulated and transferred to the graph.

For example: the simple lens equation $1/v + 1/u = 1/f$ will yield a straight line if $1/v$ is plotted as ordinate against $1/u$ as abscissa. The gradient is -1 and the intercept (on either axis, here) is $1/f$.

The equation for the adiabatic expansion of a gas, $PV^\gamma = C$ can be written in linear form by taking logs to base 10:

$$\log_{10} P + \gamma\log_{10} V = \log_{10} C.$$

A straight line is then obtained with $\log_{10} P$ as ordinate and $\log_{10} V$ as abscissa. The gradient is $-\gamma$ and intercept on the $\log_{10} P$ axis is $\log_{10} C$.

In plotting the graph make full use of the paper but avoid choosing awkward scales. Use a sharp, hard pencil and do not compound experimental errors by careless plotting. It may sometimes be undesirable to start the x-axis from zero, in which case the intercept, c, may be obtained by measuring the gradient, m, and substituting the co-ordinates (x, y) of a point on the line into the equation $y = mx + c$.

If you deduce a numerical result, record this to a sensible number of significant figures. Do not claim more accuracy than your graph or the experimental measurements allow. Note any unusual features of the graph. Is its gradient greater than theory suggests? Does it miss the origin when the quantities plotted are expected to be directly proportional? Try to suggest possible experimental causes for such features.

1 Estimation of the energy gap of germanium

Simplified theory gives the resistance–temperature relation for an intrinsic semiconductor as

$$R = A \exp(E_g/2kT) \tag{1}$$

where R is the resistance at temperature T on the kelvin scale,
   E_g is the value of the energy gap,
   k is Boltzmann's constant (8.625×10^{-5} eV K^{-1}, or 1.381×10^{-23} J K^{-1}),
and A is a constant.
   A germanium thermistor was connected to a low-voltage supply via a potential divider. The potential difference across the thermistor was measured by a valve voltmeter and the current drawn read from a milliammeter (see Figure 1.1). The thermistor unit (painted with insulating varnish) was immersed in a thermostatted water-bath.

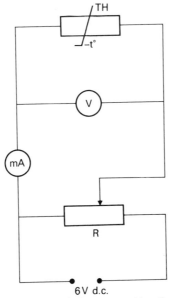

Figure 1.1 Determination of V/I for germanium thermistor.

A range of values of current and p.d. were obtained at each of several temperatures and the mean value of the resistance of the thermistor calculated at each temperature (see Table 1.1).

Table 1.1

Temperature (°C)	Resistance (ohms)
10.5	4 570
22.0	2 398
33.5	1 365
42.6	908
51.0	631
60.7	437
71.0	302
79.0	228
91.8	149

Questions

1 Rearrange equation (1) to show that $\log_{10}R = (B/T) + C$, where B and C are constants.

2 Hence determine the energy gap of germanium from a suitable linear graph.

3 Explain why a valve voltmeter or similar high-impedance instrument is used to measure the p.d. across the thermistor.

4 What would you consider to be the major sources of error in this experiment, and how could they be reduced?

5 Explain carefully the significance of the energy gap in semiconductor operation.

6 Explain why metals have positive temperature coefficients of resistivity and semiconductors have negative coefficients.

7 Describe how a thermistor can be used to protect a circuit component against current overloads, indicating where it would be connected with respect to the component it is protecting.

2 Variation with temperature of the saturation vapour pressure of water

The saturation vapour pressure of a liquid at its boiling point is equal to the pressure of the atmosphere to which it is exposed. Hence, the variation of vapour pressure with temperature can be measured by varying the external pressure and observing the corresponding variation in boiling point.

With reference to Figure 2.1, distilled water was heated in a flask fitted with an efficient reflux condenser and a fine air-leak. The pressure above the

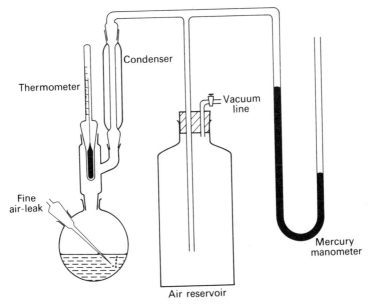

Figure 2.1 Experimental arrangement.

water was varied by means of a vacuum line attached to the tap on the air reservoir. The pressure was reduced to about two-fifths normal atmospheric pressure and the flask warmed until the water boiled. When the thermometer and manometer had settled down, the values of boiling point

(T) and difference in height of the mercury levels (h) were measured; this latter being a measure of the reduction in pressure. This process was repeated for a series of pressures and a set of values of T and h were obtained.

Table 2.1

Barometric pressure = 762 mmHg

h (mmHg)	T (K)
468	347.0
413	351.3
330	356.0
290	359.0
267	360.5
240	362.0
202	364.2
173	365.7
146	366.8
110	368.0
88	369.5
65	370.4
30	372.5
0	373.3

Questions

1   Plot a graph of saturation vapour pressure, p, against temperature, T, and comment on the shape of the curve.
(N.B. $p = 762 - h$.)

2   Plot a graph of $\log_{10}p$ as ordinate against $1/T$ as abscissa. Measure and record the gradient of the line.

3   The Clapeyron–Clausius equation, when combined with the ideal equation of state, and applied to the saturated vapour of a liquid, can be written

$$\frac{d}{dT}(\ln p) = L_v/(RT^2)$$

where p is the saturation vapour pressure of the liquid at temperature T,
       L_v is the molar latent heat of vaporization of the liquid,
and R is the molar gas constant (8.31 J mol^{-1} K^{-1}).
Hence,

$$\ln p = \int (L_v/RT^2)\, dT$$
$$= (-L_v/RT) + C$$

where C is a constant.

Thus,

$$2.303 \log_{10}p = (-L_v/RT) + C.$$

Using the slope of your graph from question 2, calculate the molar latent heat of vaporization of water.

4   Given that the molecular weight of water is 18, calculate the specific latent heat of vaporization of water.

5   What basic assumptions must be made in order to apply the Clapeyron–Clausius equation to this system? Would you consider these assumptions to be reasonable?

6   Explain carefully why the value of the latent heats calculated from the Clapeyron–Clausius equation is independent of the units in which the vapour pressure has been measured.

7   With reference to Figure 2.1 explain the functions of the following components of the apparatus:
   (a) air reservoir
   (b) reflux condenser
   (c) fine air-leak

8   Why is the thermometer bulb arranged to be above the surface of the water in the flask?

9   Sketch two curves on the same axes to show how the graph of SVP against temperature for pure water is modified when a substance is dissolved in the water. State clearly the effect of the solute on the normal boiling point of the water.

3 Variation of the refractive index of glass with wavelength of light

The refractive index, n, of a medium varies in a regular manner with the wavelength, λ, of the light used. The variation can be represented to a high degree of accuracy by Cauchy's equation,

$$n = A + (B/\lambda^2)$$

where A and B are constants for the medium concerned.

Using a spectrometer and the method of minimum deviation, the refractive index of a $60°$ glass prism was determined for seven prominent lines in the spectrum of a mercury vapour lamp.

Observations:

Table 3.1

Wavelength, λ (nm)	Refractive index, n
577.0	1.621
546.1	1.625
496.0	1.631
491.4	1.632
434.9	1.642
407.8	1.650
404.7	1.652

Questions

1 Plot a suitable linear graph and from it determine for the glass the values of A and B in Cauchy's equation.

2 Values of refractive index are commonly quoted with respect to the yellow sodium D-line, wavelength 589.0 nm. Use Cauchy's equation to calculate the refractive index of the glass for this wavelength.

3 Explain briefly what measurements are made with the spectrometer when determining the refractive index of the glass by the method of minimum

deviation. Indicate how the value of refractive index is calculated from the measurements.

4 In general, three main adjustments must be made to the components of a spectrometer before measurements are taken. Explain the importance of these adjustments and how they are carried out.

5 Sketch the paths through the prism of red and blue light incident in the same direction on the prism.

6 Calculate the angle of incidence on the 60° prism, for the sodium line of wavelength 589.0 nm, when the emergent ray is just extinguished.

4 The Helmholtz resonator

The observations in Table 4.1 represent the volume of air contained in a narrow-necked 500 ml bottle which resonates with a tuning fork of given frequency.

Assuming that changes in the air in the neck take place adiabatically, the effect can be described by the equation

$$f^n V = C \qquad (1)$$

where V is the volume of air in resonance with a fork of frequency f, and n and C are constants.

Table 4.1

f (Hz)	V (cm^3)
256	467.5
288	369.7
320	299.5
341.3	263.1
384	208.0———
426.6	168.5
480	133.0
512	117.0

Questions

1 By plotting a suitable linear graph, find the values of the constants n and C in equation (1).

2 What are the units and dimensions of the constant C in equation (1)?

3 Describe how you would carry out the experiment, paying particular attention to practical detail.

4 Point out the sources of error in your experiment and state how they can be minimized.

5 Discuss the validity of the assumption that changes in the air in the neck take place adiabatically.

5 The Zener diode

The characteristic of a silicon Zener diode at 25 °C was obtained by using the test circuit shown in Figure 5.1. The current–voltage readings are reproduced in Table 5.1.

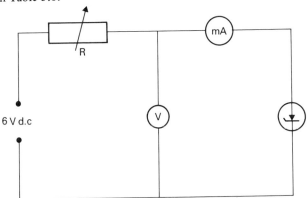

Figure 5.1 Circuit to investigate diode characteristic.

Table 5.1

Forward Bias		Reverse Bias	
V (volts)	I (mA)	V (volts)	I (mA)
0	0		
0.5	1.5	0.5	0
1.0	4.0	1.0	0.1
1.5	8.2	1.5	0.5
2.0	13.0	2.0	1.0
2.5	17.5	2.5	1.4
3.0	23.3	3.0	2.1
3.5	30.1	3.5	2.9
4.0	39.8	4.0	4.6
4.5	50.0	4.5	7.0
		4.7	9.5
		4.8	14.0
		5.0	30.0
		5.2	50.5

Questions

1 Plot the current–voltage characteristic of this p–n junction diode.

2 Discuss the shape of the curve. Account for its features in terms of electron-hole movement paying particular attention to the Zener effect and the avalanche effect.

3 Would you expect any significant changes in the characteristic if the temperature were raised to, say, 100 °C?

4 Explain, with the aid of a circuit diagram, how the Zener diode can be used to regulate or stabilize the voltage across a circuit component.

6 Formation of Newton's rings

With the experimental arrangement as shown in Figure 6.1 the optical system was illuminated by light from a sodium vapour lamp. The fringe system caused by interference at the air-film between the lens and the

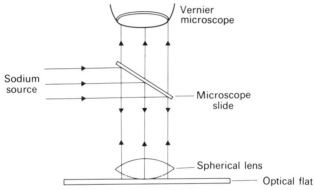

Figure 6.1 Formation of Newton's rings between lower spherical surface of lens and optical flat.

optical flat was viewed normally, and the diameters of successive bright fringes were measured with the vernier microscope. See Table 6.1.

Questions

1 Obtain the equation for the diameter D_n of the nth bright ring,

$$D_n^2 = 4R(n + \tfrac{1}{2})\lambda ,$$

where R is the radius of curvature of the spherical lower surface of the lens, and λ is the wavelength of the monochromatic light.

2 Plot a suitable linear graph and calculate the radius of curvature, R, of the lower lens surface, given that $\lambda = 589.0$ nm.

3 Comment on any unusual features of the graph and suggest possible reasons.

Table 6.1

Fringe order n	Diameter of nth bright fringe D_n (mm)
1	1.16
2	1.61
3	1.97
4	2.27
5	2.53
6	2.74
7	2.96
8	3.17
9	3.37
10	3.55
11	3.69
12	3.86
13	4.04
14	4.18
15	4.30
16	4.45

4 Explain carefully what would be observed in the microscope
   (a) if the lens were slowly lifted clear of the flat,
   (b) if the sodium lamp were replaced by a source of white light, the lens
        remaining in contact with the flat.

5 Describe one possible practical application which depends on the formation of Newton's rings.

7 Resonance in an L,C,R series circuit

An inductor (L), a capacitor (C), and a variable resistor (R) were connected so as to form a series circuit with an a.c. milliammeter. This circuit could be induced to oscillate by placing the flat-wound inductor (L) back-to-back with a similar coil connected to an audio-frequency signal generator (see Figure 7.1).

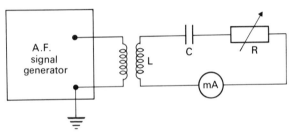

Figure 7.1 L,C,R series circuit.

With R set to zero the frequency in the primary circuit was varied until the current registered was a maximum in the secondary series circuit. This gives the resonant frequency, f_0, of the L,C,R circuit. The frequency, f, of the signal generator was then varied in 50-Hz steps on either side of f_0 and the corresponding current, I, recorded. This procedure was repeated with R set to 400 and 600 ohms in turn, so that the effect of increasing the resistance in the L,C,R circuit could be investigated.

Questions

1 Plot frequency response curves (I against f) for the three values of R on the the same set of axes.

2 Discuss the shapes of the three curves, clearly describing the effect of increasing the resistance in the series circuit.

3 Derive an expression for the impedance, Z, of the series circuit in terms of the resistance, R, and X_L, X_C, the reactance of the inductor and capacitor respectively.

Table 7.1

Inductance $L = 250$ mH, Capacitance $C = 0.1$ μF

f (kHz)	$R = 0$ I (mA)	$R = 400\Omega$ I (mA)	$R = 600\Omega$ I (mA)
0.62	8.0	7.0	6.6
0.67	10.0	8.9	8.0
0.72	12.2	10.5	9.8
0.77	15.5	12.2	11.0
0.82	19.5	14.5	12.5
0.87	24.0	16.5	14.0
0.92	29.0	18.4	15.2
0.97	32.0	19.9	16.4
1.02	33.2	20.2	17.0
1.07	32.2	20.1	17.0
1.12	30.2	20.0	16.9
1.17	28.0	19.9	16.8
1.22	26.0	19.4	16.7
1.27	24.0	18.7	16.6
1.32	22.5	18.0	16.2
1.37	21.0	17.5	15.9
1.42	20.0	16.8	15.4
1.47	19.0	16.2	15.0

4 Show that the resonant frequency f_0 is given by

$$f_0 = 1/2\pi\sqrt{(LC)}$$

and, using the values of L and C given above, compare the theoretical value of f_0 for the circuit with that from the curves.

5 Explain carefully how an L,C,R circuit can be used in a radio receiver for coupling the aerial circuit to the input of the first stage. Indicate how the receiver is tuned to transmitting stations of different frequencies, and describe how the resistance of the circuit affects the tuning capabilities.

8 Use of de Sauty bridge to measure relative permittivity

Alternating-current bridge circuits can be used to compare impedances of components in a similar way to the comparison of resistances by d.c. (Wheatstone bridge) circuits.

Consider the De Sauty bridge shown in Figure 8.1. The bridge supply is drawn from a sinusoidal signal generator instead of a cell, and the balance detector is a cathode ray oscilloscope instead of a galvanometer.

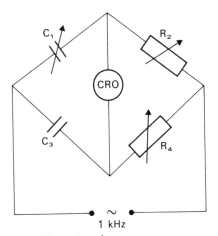

Figure 8.1 De Sauty bridge network.

At balance, the impedances of the components are related by an equation similar to that between the resistances in the arms of a Wheatstone bridge.

$$\frac{Z_1}{Z_2} = \frac{Z_3}{Z_4}.$$

With the components shown, this becomes

$$\frac{X_1}{R_2} = \frac{X_3}{R_4}$$

where X_1, X_3 are the reactances of the capacitors C_1 and C_3, and this equation can be rearranged to give the balance condition

$$\frac{C_3}{C_1} = \frac{R_2}{R_4}. \tag{1}$$

In the experiment R_2 and R_4 were decade resistance boxes of negligible inductance; C_3 was a standard capacitor and C_1 a variable, parallel-plate capacitor. This was composed of a series of interleaved metal plates pivoted on a common axis so that the area of overlap of the surfaces could be varied. The variable capacitor (in a glass container) was used fully closed, i.e. maximum area of overlap, first with air between the plates. By observing the trace on the CRO a series of pairs of values of R_2 and R_4 for which the bridge was balanced was obtained.

The experiment was repeated with the variable capacitor totally immersed in cyclohexane, taking care to exclude all air from between the plates; and another set of values of R_2 and R_4 obtained for balance.

Table 8.1

C_1 in air		C_1 in cyclohexane	
R_2 (Ω)	R_4 (Ω)	R_2 (Ω)	R_4 (Ω)
990	600	500	600
870	500	420	500
750	450	380	450
660	400	340	400
580	350	290	350
500	300	250	300
420	250	210	250
330	200	160	200
250	150	130	150
170	100	80	100
80	50	40	50

Questions

1 From the given balance condition obtain equation (1).

2 Given that the capacitance of a parallel-plate capacitor,

$$C = \frac{\epsilon A}{4\pi D}$$

where ϵ is the permittivity of the medium between the plates,
    A is the area of the plates,
and D is the separation of the plates,

show that the relative permittivity, ϵ_r, of cyclohexane can be obtained from the equation

$$\epsilon_r = \frac{S_a}{S_c}$$

where S_a and S_c are respectively the gradients of the lines obtained by plotting R_2 against R_4 for air and for cyclohexane as the capacitor dielectric.

3   Plot the suggested graphs and calculate the relative permittivity ϵ_r of cyclohexane.

4   Sketch the appearance of the trace you would expect to observe on the oscilloscope screen when the bridge is (a) unbalanced, and (b) balanced exactly.

5   The galvanometer used to detect the balance point in a d.c. bridge usually has a high resistance in series to protect the instrument. This is shorted out near balance to provide greater sensitivity of the galvanometer. How would you vary the sensitivity of the CRO used in the a.c. bridge?

6   Why is it essential to the accuracy of the experiment that the windings of the resistance boxes should have as low an inductance as possible?

7   All values of R_2 and R_4 were read to the nearest 10 ohms because of lack of sensitivity of the CRO in detecting small deviations from the balance point. How would you expect this to affect the accuracy of the values of resistance recorded, and the accuracy of the experiment as a whole?

9 Conduction of heat along an unlagged metal bar

Consider an unlagged copper bar heated at one end by a steam chest (Figure 9.1).

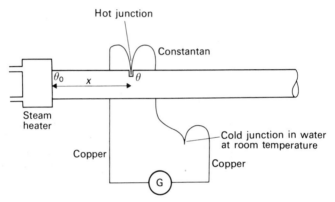

Figure 9.1 Arrangement for observing temperature distribution along bar.

If θ is the excess temperature over the surroundings at a distance x from the heated end, then theory shows that, in the steady state

$$\theta = \theta_0 \exp(-bx) \qquad (1)$$

where $\theta = \theta_0$ when $x = 0$, and b is a constant depending on the dimensions and material of the bar.

When steady state conditions had been attained, the excess temperature θ was measured for several distances x by means of a copper-constantan thermocouple connected to a scalamp galvanometer; the hot junction being placed in each of a series of small holes drilled at intervals along the bar, and the cold junction kept in a beaker of water at room temperature. The excess temperature θ was recorded in terms of the number of millimetre-divisions registered on the galvanometer scale (see Table 9.1).

Table 9.1

x (cm)	θ (mm)
1.0	217
6.2	167
12.3	123
19.3	105
27.2	77
37.2	52
49.2	36
63.3	20
79.3	11
97.3	5
115.2	3

Questions

1 Plot a suitable linear graph to verify that the temperature distribution along the bar obeys equation (1).

2 Measure the gradient of the line. Hence calculate the value of b and give its units.

3 Draw a sketch of the curve you would expect to obtain if θ were plotted as ordinate against x as abscissa.

4 What is meant by 'in the steady state'?

5 Why is the cold junction of the thermocouple kept at room temperature, rather than in melting ice at $0\,^{\circ}C$?

6 Why is it sufficient in the experiment to record the excess temperature θ in terms of the galvanometer deflection?

7 Describe the procedure you would follow to calibrate the thermocouple system if the excess temperatures were required in degrees Celsius.

8 In what way will the introduction of the thermojunction modify the flow of heat through the bar? Would it be better to measure the temperature on the surface so as to avoid making holes in the bar?

9 What factors, apart from the excess temperature, will determine the rate at which heat is lost to the air from the bar?

10 Absorption of gamma- and beta-radiation

The absorption of gamma- and beta-radiation by metals was investigated in each case for absorbers of increasing thickness interposed between the collimated source and a Geiger-Muller tube.

The sources used were cobalt-60 (for gamma) and strontium-90 (for beta) in conjunction with lead and aluminium absorbers respectively, supplied by Panax.

In the tables of observations the density of the absorbing medium is taken into account by expressing the absorber thickness, d, in terms of the surface density of the absorber.

Thus, absorber thickness = density x thickness, and the units of d are therefore kg m^{-2}.

Table 10.1 Absorption of gamma-radiation by lead

Absorber thickness, d. (kg m^{-2})	Corrected count rate, C. (cps)
0 (in air)	22.9
36	20.8
72	18.3
107	13.7
143	11.6
179	10.6
215	8.0
250	6.8
286	5.5
322	5.1
357	4.2

The G—M tube was used with a scaler and the count rate calculated and corrected for background radiation. The counting time was 60 seconds throughout the gamma-absorption experiment but was gradually increased to as long as 10 minutes towards the end of the beta-absorption experiment.

Table 10.2 Absorption of beta-radiation by aluminium

Absorber thickness, d. (kg m^{-2})	Corrected count rate, C. (cps)
0 (in air)	94.6
0.92	86.5
1.35	70.6
1.65	65.4
2.15	50.4
3.40	26.6
5.05	10.2
6.15	5.35
7.55	1.43
9.25	0.334
9.95	0.108
11.25	0.055
12.25	0.038
12.95	0.035
13.95	0.030

Questions

1 Using semi-logarithmic paper plot graphs of count rate (log axis) against absorber thickness (linear axis) for each table of observations.

2 Assuming that the graph of gamma-absorption can be described by the equation $C = C_0 \exp(-\mu d)$, where C is the count rate for absorber thickness d, obtain the value of μ from the graph.

3 What do the symbols μ and C_0 represent in this equation?

4 Under what experimental conditions could the count rate C be assumed to be proportional to the intensity of the gamma radiation?

5 Sketch the shape of the graph you would expect to obtain for gamma absorption if count rate is plotted against absorber thickness on ordinary linear graph paper.

6 What is the possible cause of the residual count rate observed for beta radiation with the thickest absorbers?

7 Estimate from the graph the maximum range (in kg m^{-2}) of the beta radiation.

8 Why is it desirable to increase the counting time towards the end of the beta-absorption experiment?

11 Hysteresis loop for a ferromagnetic specimen

Using the experimental arrangement shown in Figure 11.1, an accurately known current was passed through the primary windings around the specimen, which was in the form of an annulus. The corresponding flux linkage in the

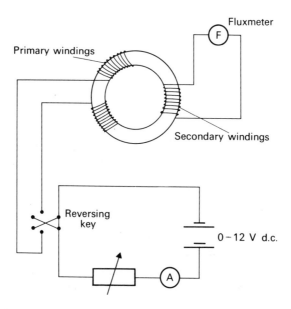

Figure 11.1 Experimental arrangement (schematic).

secondary windings was read from the fluxmeter. From a knowledge of the dimensions of the annulus and the number of turns in the primary and secondary coils, the magnetizing field (H) and the induced flux density (B) in the annulus were calculated from the readings of primary current and flux linkage respectively.

Before taking readings, the hysteresis cycle was traversed four or five times in the direction ACEFA; see sketch of loop, Figure 11.2. Then starting

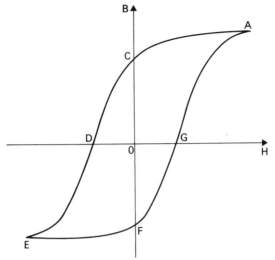

Figure 11.2 Sketch of hysteresis loop.

from point A in the cycle, the following values of magnetizing field (*H*) and flux density (*B*) were obtained:

Table 11.1

Point on curve	H $(kA\ m^{-1})$	B (tesla)
A	2.098	1.354
	0.981	1.260
	0.708	1.218
	0.294	1.090
	0.079	0.976
C	0.000	0.927
	−0.084	0.857
	−0.301	−0.186
	−0.718	−1.028
	−0.997	−1.148
E	−2.098	−1.354
	−0.981	−1.260
	−0.708	−1.218
	−0.294	−1.090
	−0.079	−0.976
F	0.000	−0.927
	0.084	−0.857
	0.301	0.186
	0.718	1.028
	0.997	1.148
A	2.098	1.354

Questions

1 Construct the hysteresis loop by plotting B as ordinate against H as abscissa.

2 Read off from the graph the values of the remanence and the coercivity of the specimen.

3 Calculate the relative permeability, μ_r, of the specimen when it is in maximum magnetizing field (point A); the permeability of free space, $\mu_0 = 4\pi \times 10^{-7} \text{ H m}^{-1}$. Why cannot μ_r be regarded as a constant for a particular ferromagnetic specimen?

4 From the shape of your curve and the quantities you have calculated, would you classify the specimen as a hard or soft magnetic material? Give reasons for your choice.

5 Suggest a practical reason for traversing the hysteresis loop several times before taking measurements and, using domain theory, describe the changes taking place in the specimen during one complete traversal of the loop.

12 Ultrasonic determination of the velocity of sound in carbon tetrachloride

In an experiment to determine the velocity of sound in carbon tetrachloride a sample of the liquid filled a parallel-sided glass cell, into one side of which was fixed a quartz-crystal transducer. The quartz crystal was connected to a high-frequency signal generator so that an ultrasonic standing wave of wavelength λ_1 was set up in the liquid by reflexion from the opposite side of the cell.

This causes the liquid in the cell to act like a diffraction grating, and when the cell was illuminated normally by a helium-neon laser, a diffraction pattern was obtained on the screen (see Figure 12.1). The separation of the diffraction maxima are recorded in Table 12.1.

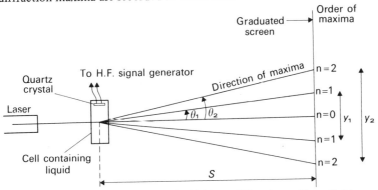

Figure 12.1 Direction of maxima formed by diffraction of laser light at ultrasonically-formed grating.

Table 12.1

Order of diffraction maxima, n	Separation of maxima, y (cm)
1	0.80
2	1.60
3	2.40
4	3.20
5	4.00
6	4.80

Constants of the apparatus:

Wavelength of laser light used, $\lambda = 6.328 \times 10^{-7}$ m
Distance from cell to screen, s $= 2.610$ m
Frequency of H.F. generator, f $= 1.140$ MHz

Questions

1 Explain the mechanism by which the diffraction grating is formed by the ultrasonic standing wave. State the relation between the wavelength λ_1 of the standing wave and the spacing, d, of the grating.

2 Show that, for normal incidence on the grating,

$$d \sin \theta = n\lambda$$

where λ is the wavelength of the laser light and θ the direction of the maxima of order n.

3 From the above equation and the geometry of Figure 12.1, show that

$$\lambda_1 y = 4ns\lambda$$

where y is the separation of the maxima of order n and s is the distance from cell to screen.
(Use the approximation that, when θ is very small, $\tan \theta = \sin \theta$.)

4 Plot a graph of y against n and so calculate the velocity, V, of sound in carbon tetrachloride.

5 The temperature of the liquid in the cell has not been recorded. State, with reasons, whether you consider this to be a serious omission.

6 What effect, if any, would you expect the dimensions of the cell to have on the position of the pattern on the screen?

7 What are the properties of laser light that make it ideally suited for this experiment?

8 What instrument would you choose to measure the distance from the cell to the screen? Justify your choice in terms of the accuracy you would expect to obtain from this experiment.

Answers to Data Analysis Papers

Test No.

1	*2.*	0.75 eV	
2	*3.*	3.91 kJ mol^{-1};	*4.* 2.17 MJ kg^{-1}
3	*1.*	1.592, 9.615 x 10^{-15} m^2 ;	
	2.	1.620; *6.* 37° 6′	
4	*1.*	2, 741 cm^3 s^{-2}	
6	*2.*	52.4 cm	
7	*4.*	1.01 kHz	
8	*3.*	2.0	
9	*2.*	42.5 m^{-1}	
10	*2.*	5.0 x 10^{-3} m^2 kg^{-1}; *7.* 10.4 kg m^{-2}	
11	*2.*	0.93 T, 0.27 kA m^{-1} ; *3.* 504	
12	*4.*	941 m s^{-1}	